The Opium Wars

A Captivating Guide to the First and Second Opium War and Their Impact on the History of the United Kingdom and China

Free Bonus from Captivating History (Available for a Limited time)

Hi History Lovers!

Now you have a chance to join our exclusive history list so you can get your first history ebook for free as well as discounts and a potential to get more history books for free! Simply visit the link below to join.

Captivatinghistory.com/ebook

Also, make sure to follow us on Facebook, Twitter and Youtube by searching for Captivating History.

Contents

Introduction

Victorian Great Britain was the most technologically and economically developed country in the world at the time. As such, it had the power to protect its interests. With the discovery of new trade routes in the East, and with the foundation of the East India Company, Britain became addicted to the luxurious and exotic items from China. Silk, porcelain, and tea were in high demand among the rich. Britain was so economically strong at the time that even the middle and lower classes could afford to enjoy high-quality items imported from China, especially tea.

Britain imported everything its society desired, but it was costly. The main problem was that China only accepted payments in silver, creating a huge imbalance in trade. To avoid losing money on imported goods, Britain had to sell something back to China. However, this Eastern empire liked to boast that it was self-sufficient. The Chinese didn't need to import anything, as their industry was developed enough to supply the whole country with what it needed. Britain had to come up with something the Chinese needed, and in desperation, the decision was made for Britain to sell opium.

With rich poppy plantations in Britain's Indian possessions, opium was abundant. It was banned in Great Britain, except when diluted in red wine in very small amounts and prescribed by doctors in the form of laudanum. Since they could not sell the drug back home, British opium merchants needed a new market. There were no better experimental grounds than China, which was just opening up to foreign trade. When diplomatic efforts to introduce opium to the Chinese market failed, the British Parliament approved an alternative: war.

There were two wars, one from 1839 to 1842 and another from 1856 to 1860. They are collectively known as the Opium Wars. The British, who were joined by French and supported by the Americans and Russians, clashed with Imperial China, which was ruled by the Qing dynasty. These conflicts are largely forgotten in the Western world, perhaps out of a sense of collective shame. But in China, the Opium Wars are still symbols of national humiliation at the hands of the Western powers.

For over 4,000 years, China believed itself to be the pinnacle of civilization, regarding other nations as barbarians who were not worthy of the imperial presence of their Son of Heaven, the emperor. As such, China's feelings of superiority often halted its diplomacy. Since the nation was stuck in tradition, it was doomed to suffer the inadequate political decisions of their emperor and his advisors. Xenophobia reached extremes when foreigners were prohibited from entering the country. Instead of opening up to other nations and learning from them, China decided to close its borders and not allow the outside world to taint their sacred society. Although the moral blame for the Opium Wars lies with Britain, the ideological blame is on China. Perhaps through less strict diplomacy, it could have found common grounds with the Western world and avoided the devastating effects of both the drug and the war.

Even though the Opium Wars were fought a century and a half ago, to modern readers, the events might seem quite contemporary. They represent a narrative that perfectly describes colonialism, which is defined by greed, power, corruption, racism, and the collective madness of a nation. The Opium Wars are a reminder for the future, as they perfectly describe what happens when two different worlds clash. The events in this book can only serve to teach us of humility, selflessness, and compassion. At the heart of the Opium Wars is the international drug trade, which we still fight even today.

Chapter 1 – Prelude - The Red Barbarians

George Macartney, 1ˢᵗ Earl Macartney
(https://en.wikipedia.org/wiki/George_Macartney,_1st_Earl_Macartne
*y#/media/File:George_Macartney,_1st_Earl_Macartney_by_Lemuel_*
Francis_Abbott.jpg)

The First Opium War began in 1839, but the first shots were fired much earlier. The trade agreement with Imperial China meant the opening of a huge market to a certain country. The custom was, out of respect, that all delegations had to bow to the Chinese emperor. However, the British delegation refused to perform this traditional act, known as "kowtow" in the Mandarin dialect. The main diplomat of the British delegation was Lord George Macartney, a person who managed to raise himself from the poverty of Ireland and enter the Foreign Service. He built his reputation and was known as a diplomat who got things done. However, China was a challenge for him.

China was culturally different from 19th-century Europe. It remains unique even today, although the differences between these modern nations are greatly lessened. Macartney arrived in China in 1793 with the task of opening up a British embassy in the capital. From there, he was to continue his diplomatic mission and persuade the Chinese emperor to allow British ships to dock in Canton and establish trade. To speed up the process, Macartney was permitted to promise the end of the opium imports from British India. In Imperial China, opium was already banned, but it was impossible to stop it from entering the empire. It was even more impossible to control the people who enjoyed it.

The previous relations between China and Britain were not good at all, and the Chinese attitude toward the newly arrived British ambassador was one of resentment. Macartney's luggage was thrown in the trash upon his arrival, and he had to travel to the capital in a barge with a displayed sign that said, "Tribute from The Red Barbarians." The humiliating journey toward Peking (Beijing) was observed by the Chinese as a tribute, and the label of European peoples as "red-haired barbarians" came from earlier times. China felt superior toward the rest of the world. They called themselves the "Middle Kingdom" or the "Central Civilization," and they were not referring to the geographical position of China. They genuinely believed they were the center around which all humanity rose.

The Chinese emperor was considered to be not of this world. His official title was the Son of Heaven and the Lord of Ten Thousand Years. He was no mere mortal who received ambassadors. The only ones allowed to approach the emperor were the tribute bearers. In the eyes of the Chinese government, Lord Macartney wasn't an ambassador or a diplomat. He bore the tribute of the British, and it was only as tribute bearer that he could step in front of the emperor. By Chinese tradition, the foreigners couldn't negotiate anything with the emperor. They were all his subjects, and as such, they came to pay their respects. This means that King George III (1760–1820) was seen as a vassal of the Qianlong Emperor (1735–1796).

It was this worldview disagreement that destined Macartney's mission to failure, not his disobedience in the kowtow ritual, as many still believe. The Qianlong Emperor agreed to a compromise and allowed Macartney to bow as if he would bow to his own king. Later, the Chinese emperor sent a letter to the British king, explaining in detail why China did not need the trade agreement or the British embassy. The Qianlong Emperor explained that he ruled over such a vast empire that it could provide his people with everything they required, so the import of goods was not needed. However, the tone of the letter was as if the Qianlong Emperor had written to his subordinate; he even urged the British king to obey him.

Even though Macartney's mission failed, and he never achieved a trade agreement with the Chinese emperor, the British diplomats came back with important information about the Chinese defenses. Among the people who accompanied Macartney were artists, whose task was to draw what they saw in the exotic cities and countryside. They brought home the drawings of various fortifications and the city's defenses, which gave Britain an insight into Chinese strengths and weaknesses. Thus, Britain used this mission to learn about China, which could be its potential enemy or ally.

Allying with China was essential to engage in trade with the far-off country. As a vast empire, China represented a huge potential market for the import and export of goods. The first trade between the Europeans and the Chinese occurred in the 16th century when the Portuguese sent their trade mission. They were soon followed by other European countries, and among them was the British East India Company, which had a royal charter to conduct trade in the Far East. At the time, Europe was the leader in industrial life, especially Britain, which managed to put a monopoly on industrial production due to the low cost of raw materials imported from the East Indies where the Company had its base. Because of this monopoly, the standard of living in Britain grew exponentially. With it, the demand for luxury and exotic goods from the Far East increased. People wanted Chinese silk, porcelain, and tea, which became the most important imported goods, ones that the British economy depended upon.

However, trade with China was imbalanced. Instead of various British goods, China wanted nothing but silver. British merchants managed to convince the Chinese government to allow the import of some raw materials, such as calico, iron, and tin. Since China boasted about its self-sufficiency, they wanted nothing European. The result was a trade deficit in Europe. Although the British had access to sources of silver through their colonies in the Americas, there was not enough silver to keep it circulating in Europe and to pay China for its goods. Britain alone paid over twenty-six million pounds for Chinese goods between 1710 and 1759 but only sold those goods for nine million pounds. To keep the economy strong, Europeans had to persuade the Chinese emperor to allow the import of goods other than silver.

But the trade with the Chinese wasn't limited only by their unwillingness to import foreign goods. China wanted to limit foreign influence, so it only allowed foreign trade through one port city: Guangzhou (Canton). The geographical location of the city was ideal for the delivery of goods, as it lay on the Pearl River Delta. However, this meant bottlenecking all trade, and the European merchants were frustrated with the time it took the Chinese officials to process their goods. They tried to persuade the emperor to allow them access to other ports but to no avail.

The Qianlong Emperor went even further to limit foreign influence in China. Europeans were only allowed to trade through thirteen official factories, all situated in Canton. They had to deal with the special Chinese traders who were directly responsible for all foreign merchants and their goods. Also, foreigners were not allowed to learn the Chinese language or to bring their women to China. They were also banned from marrying the locals or traveling inland without special permission from the emperor himself. The collection of laws that concerned foreign policy and trade was known as the "Prevention of Barbarian Ordinances," and they were set forth by the Qianlong Emperor of the Qing dynasty, who explained that China was healthy and that it had no need for inferior foreign products. He also stated that even if China opened up to foreign trade in the future, foreigners would not be allowed into the nation.

Breaking into the Chinese market was almost impossible. So, to keep up with the pace of the economy, Britain had to find something China wanted more than silver. The answer was pretty simple. To gain more from the Chinese, the European traders had to circumvent the official trade network and engage in the lucrative black market of the opium trade. Importing opium to China was illegal, but the emperor did not have enough power to fight it. Opium brought enough profit for the local Chinese trade officials to keep silent about it and send it through the underground channels of the black market.

Opium wasn't new in China. It was first brought by Arab merchants of the Middle Ages who cultivated it in Asia Minor. But opium was used as a medicine back then, as it is a powerful analgesic. Dysentery was the most common disease in the Middle Ages, and opium was often the prescribed remedy because it had the beneficial side-effect of causing constipation. In the 17th century, the opium trade continued through Dutch and French merchants, and it was picked up by the British in the 18th century. Europeans had vast opium plantations in their Indian colonies. They used much of the arable land in India to produce plenty of opium but not enough food. This, in turn, caused famine to rage through the Indian subcontinent. But the profit from selling opium was good enough to keep the machinery going.

At first, the British East India Company tried to prevent its officials from indulging in the illegal opium trade in China because it interfered with their legal business. However, due to China's strict laws regarding foreign policy, the financial reality was that the Company simply had to give in to be able to survive the competitive market in the East. The American Revolution cut off Britain from its sources of silver, and it needed to find other means of keeping the trade in the East alive to supply its citizens with the highly demanded Chinese goods.

In 1782, the first British ships were sent to China with a cargo of 3,450 chests of opium, with each chest containing 170 pounds. Two ships set sail, but one was captured by the French. The other one reached Macau in southern China. There, they tried to sell opium to any Chinese buyer, but no one wanted it. China was not yet the nation of addicts. The highest price the British got for their opium was in Malaysia, where a chest was sold for the value of 340 in today's US dollars, even though its real value was around 500 dollars. The Company was stuck in a losing battle.

This didn't stop the East India Company to continue trying, and in only fifteen years, the Chinese demand for opium was so high that they imported over a thousand chests filled with the drug annually. In 1799, the Chinese emperor had to enforce the ban of opium more strictly, as the nation widely indulged in the vice. The British East India Company supported the emperor officially, and it even stopped importing the drug to China. However, in India, they continued selling it to the independent merchants, British or foreign, who continued selling it on the Chinese black market.

Opium alone brought 39,000 pounds to the Company in 1773. Such a huge profit couldn't be ignored. In India, they sold opium for four times the price of poppies, which was the raw material opium was derived from. Twenty years later, the revenue opium brought to the Company was estimated at 250,000 pounds. And this was just the beginning of normalizing the trade balance between China and Britain. Between 1806 and 1809, China paid seven million silver dollars for opium. This wasn't nearly enough to cover the amount Britain spent on Chinese goods, but it was a start. The opium addiction in the empire continued to grow, and the demand for the drug increased very quickly. Since the British East India Company had a monopoly on the Indian production of the drug, it could continue artificially raising its price. During the early 19th century, Britain started selling over 5,000 chests of opium. The increase in demand was enough to balance out the trade between the two nations.

But no matter how much opium the British East India Company sold to the Chinese, it was still bottlenecked in Canton, which was the only port opened to foreigners. This meant the drug couldn't sell fast enough, and Britain knew it needed more ports on the Chinese coast. This was why they sent another mission to the Chinese emperor in 1816. The leader of the new mission was William Amherst, and the Chinese emperor was Qianlong's successor, the Jiaqing Emperor (1796–1820). But this mission was an utter failure, and the British ambassador never even got to see the emperor. Just like his predecessor Macartney, Lord Amherst refused to perform the kowtow ritual, unless the same kind of respect was shown to the British king by Chinese court officials. For this, he was denied entry into Peking, and he had to turn his ship around and return to Britain.

Over the next twenty years, the number of imported opium chests to China grew to 18,000 annually. Only three years later, this number soared to 30,000. China became the nation of opium addicts, and the demand for the drug was extremely high. Everyone was a consumer at this point. While opium was the drug of the elite at the beginning of the 18th century, the mid-19th century saw the drug reaching even the lowest, poorest members of Chinese society. Even Taoist priests and soldiers were giving in to this vice.

British Parliament abolished the monopoly the East India Company had in China to allow other independent merchants access to the empire's market. However, the Chinese authorities didn't want to deal with each merchant individually, and they demanded Britain to appoint one person who could be held accountable for all British trade in China. Parliament agreed that British authority had to be established in Canton, and the new office of chief superintendent of trade was opened. The first to occupy this office was Lord William Napier. His task was not just to protect British trade interests but also to try and open up more port cities to British vessels and an embassy in Peking.

Upon his arrival in Canton, Napier failed to meet with the viceroy of Liangguang, Lu Kun, who insisted on going through the official channels of the Cohong, the guild of Chinese merchants, as they were the only ones allowed to petition the viceroy. Napier was ordered to go to Macau, where he was to wait for the tea season. Only then would he be allowed entry into Canton, just like any other foreign trader. On top of that, Viceroy Lu Kun ordered a halt with all British traders to force Napier's retreat to Macau. Lord Napier moved to Macau, but he was so infuriated with the treatment he received in Canton that he believed the only solution to opening up trade in China was through the use of force.

The independent British traders advocated for a military solution when they saw the diplomatic missions fail. Under their influence, Napier wrote a letter to the British Parliament, asking for their support in an attack on China. However, Parliament wasn't willing to go to war when there was still a chance the matter could be settled diplomatically. But Napier dared to approach the Chinese people of Canton with ideas of war, and he was accused of turning them against their government. For this, the British were ordered to leave Canton and go to Macau, although American, Dutch, and French traders could stay and continue their businesses.

Angered, Lord Napier sent two British frigates, the *Imogen* and *Andromache*, to Whampoa, where he knew the British ships would be attacked by the Chinese. He ordered the captains to return fire and destroy the Chinese fort at Whampoa on September 11th, 1834. The first exchange of volleys showed how weak the Chinese defenses were. The fort only had stationary cannons and could not aim. Their only option was to shoot above and beyond the British ships. From a safe distance, the two frigates returned fire, knocking out all sixty of the fort's cannons. It was there, at the Bocca Tigris, a narrow strait in the Pearl River Delta near Humen, that the first exchange of fire, a prelude to the First Opium War.

Although it was the British who broke the Chinese law and sailed where they were not allowed, Lord Napier used the Chinese response as an excuse to escalate the conflict. The Chinese blocked the way of the frigates with stone barges and fire rafts, which would cause extreme damage if they came into contact with British ships loaded with gunpowder. However, before he could deepen the conflict, Napier became sick with typhus. Feverish, he had to return to Macau, where he would receive better medical care. Unfortunately, he died there on October 11th.

Lord Napier's efforts had no support back home in Britain. He was mocked for his diplomatic tactics, which were promptly named "Napier's Fizzle." However, British merchants in China had a different view. They were impatient, and their businesses couldn't wait for Parliament to succeed with its diplomatic ways. They thought a war would grant them access to the Chinese market because surely the British would win against such a backward enemy whose defenses hadn't been updated in centuries. So, merchants signed a petition to King William IV, demanding military intervention.

In 1836, the Daoguang Emperor (1820–1850) issued another proclamation banning the trade of opium. However, just like the proclamation of the previous emperor, this one was ignored. The rumor was that the viceroy of Canton was involved in the opium trade, so once another proclamation was issued ordering all foreign traders to leave China, it was completely ignored. But it wasn't just Viceroy Deng Tingzhen who benefited from opium. The government of China was thoroughly corrupted, and the officials of the imperial court were often involved in the opium trade, either through smuggling or through bribes paid for the safe passage of opium.

But the Daoguang Emperor wouldn't tolerate his people indulging in opium addiction, and he wanted to end the illegal trade of it. The exact number of the Chinese opium addicts is not known, but modern scholars estimate anywhere between four and twelve million. Most of them were young men in their prime years, between twenty and fifty-five. This is when they should have been the most productive, and instead of tending to their families, they were wasting their days in opium dens. Viceroy Deng was ordered to do something, but he couldn't strike at the foreigners, as they were the main source of his income (through taxes and bribes). Instead, he chose to punish Chinese opium traders. All around the country, smugglers, sellers, buyers, and addicts were arrested. Some of them were executed as an example to the others.

Chapter 2 – No Tolerance

View of the foreign quarter in Canton

(https://en.wikipedia.org/wiki/First_Opium_War#/media/File:AMH-6145-NA_View_of_Canton.jpg)

The Chinese government continued to fight the opium trade by suppressing the import of it. Unfortunately for them, the results were weak, so the emperor called his governors to try and resolve the opium problem once and for all. Various state officials were gathered to give their advice, but all of them had a different stance on the problem. Some urged the emperor to legalize and decriminalize it so he could collect the tax on its trade and transport, which would bring enormous profits to the royal treasury. Others were completely against it, and they insisted on punishing the traders and addicts. After hearing all sides, the Daoguang Emperor made the final decision. He opted for the total suppression of opium, taking the advice of the loudest speaker against the drug, Lin Zexu, the viceroy of Hubei and Hunan provinces.

Lin Zexu's nickname was "Blue Sky" because of his morality. People often said he was as pure as the cloudless sky. Besides his moral values, the emperor praised his viceroy for managing to exterminate the trade and use of opium from Hubei and Hunan. Lin was a literary scholar and an avid reformer of the empire. As he grew up, he witnessed the nation being destroyed by opium addiction, and he wanted to cleanse the empire from this plague. Lin built his career as a diplomat and was often tasked with resolving very complicated matters.

In 1839, Lin Zexu was sent to Canton, the point where the drug entered the country and moved inward. As soon as he arrived, he wrote an open letter to Queen Victoria (1819-1901), asking her to ban the opium trade. He noted that China traded luxury items, such as silk, tea, and porcelain, with Britain, and all it received in return was the poison of opium. He alluded to the queen's nobility, urging her to act against the British merchants who lacked common sense and morals. Lin's letter was published in Canton for everyone to see. In it, he asked the British queen:

> They may not intend to harm others on purpose, but the fact remains that they are so obsessed with material gain that they have no concern whatever for the harm they can cause to others. Have they no conscience? I have heard that you strictly prohibit opium in your own country, indicating unmistakably that you know how harmful opium is. You do not wish opium to harm your own country, but you choose to bring that harm

to other countries such as China. Why? (Lin Wen-Chung Kung cheng-shu, vol. 2, roll 3.)

Even though the letter was later printed in the London *Times*, Lin Zexu never received a reply. To the Chinese, Lin issued edicts, urging everyone to stop and report opium smugglers. He also asked teachers to set an example for their students and abstain from the drug. Lin even asked the Medical Missionary Society to recommend a supplement drug that would help people overcome their addiction. He genuinely believed people could be rehabilitated. However, he punished the opium users who couldn't stop consuming the drug after eighteen months. They had to be executed to set an example and provide motivation for the others.

The emperor of China accepted the rehabilitation attempt of Lin Zexu. The measures were harsh. All foreign importers of opium were to be beheaded, while Chinese traders were to be strangled. The death penalty awaited any government official who turned a blind eye to the opium trade or, even worse, accepted bribes for it. By the spring of 1839, 1,600 people in Canton were arrested, from dealers to opium den owners to addicts. Forty thousand opium pipes were seized, and one thousand opium chests were confiscated and destroyed. By the summer of that same year, 11,000 more opium chests were found in foreign ships and burned.

The British opium traders publicly announced they were stopping the illegal opium trade, seemingly bending to the Chinese laws. To show their goodwill, they even agreed to hand over 1,000 opium chests to authorities. In reality, they continued the trade using different contacts. The ships loaded with drugs from India would now stop in Singapore instead of Canton, and from there, the Chinese smugglers would take over. But the foreigners could not fool Lin Zexu. He saw their ruse and ordered the arrest of one of the most prominent British traders, Matthew Jardine, who had no choice but to flee to Singapore.

To further fight the opium trade, the Chinese government had to stop the middleman, the Cohong, as its members were the only ones allowed to buy from and sell to foreigners. Over time, they took part in the opium trade and grew very rich. They even supplied the British with wooden chests in which they would transport opium from India. To pay for the drug, the Cohong used the empire's silver reserves, and they cut the riches of the royal treasury in half. The Chinese government not only publicly accused them of conspiring against the nation with foreign traders, but they also ordered the Cohong to give up all the information they had on their foreign partners. Instead of sentencing them to death, Lin Zexu tasked the Cohong to bring him all the opium they received from their foreign contacts. If they failed to do so, in three days, they were to be arrested, and their wealth and lands were to be confiscated so that their families would be shamed.

The Cohong notified their foreign contacts of Lin's orders, and the merchants asked for time so they could have a meeting and discuss Lin's threats. They came up with the reply that the contraband was not theirs to turn over to the Chinese officials. It belonged to the factories of India, and they were just ensuring the merchandise reached its destination. They just wanted to keep their profits by any means, and they didn't seem to care that their Chinese partners, the Cohong, would lose their lives. The refusal of the foreign traders to surrender the opium instigated Lin's next response. He confiscated all the opium aboard the British ship *Snipe* by force. The crews of the ships near Canton were also placed under house arrest.

In 1839, the new chief superintendent of trade, Charles Elliot, set sail for Canton from Macau. He ordered all British ships to retreat to the safety of Hong Kong. Before the merchants could leave the foreign quarter of Canton, it was besieged by the Chinese army. Lin Zexu simply couldn't allow them to refuse to surrender the opium and run to Hong Kong or anywhere outside of Chinese authority. Afraid of a food shortage, Charles Elliot wrote to Lin, asking for permission to negotiate. The next morning, Lin demanded that all the opium be surrendered at once. Elliot had no other choice but to capitulate. He ordered the British traders to surrender the drug, but he also promised them compensation for the loss by the British government. However, he had no authorization to make such a promise. The merchants were happy to get the troublesome opium out of their hands and leave Canton as soon as possible. They turned all of their possessions in, hoping that the British Parliament would pay them back.

But the surrender of the contraband did not result in the release of the British merchants. Lin ordered the gates of the foreign quarter to be sealed, inspiring fear in its inhabitants. Lin didn't just want the opium from the British; he wanted all the opium. He was still waiting on American and Indian merchants to surrender their stocks. At the time, there were no French traders in Canton, and the Dutch had already stopped the opium trade by this time. The Americans and Indians continued to claim they were not the owners of the drug; therefore, they could not simply give it up. But to the Chinese, all foreigners were the same. They were barbarians who stuck together, and even if they didn't trade the drug directly, they were still supporting their colleagues.

Finally, on May 21ˢᵗ, all the merchants of the foreign quarter agreed to give up their opium under the condition that Lin allowed them to perform the transport. A portion of foreigners had to stay in the city under lockdown until the drugs reached their destination on the island of Chuenpi. Lin was victorious in his efforts to cleanse Canton of opium, and Indian factories took it as a sign that the Chinese market was closed forever. The price of opium dropped from the previous $600 to only $200 per chest.

Finally, the lockdown of the foreigners was over, and Lin allowed fifty of them to leave China, as everyone was not allowed to leave. Those who were considered main opium traders had to remain in close vicinity of Lin Zexu until he made sure no opium was illegally imported into China. On May 24ᵗʰ, finally satisfied, Lin ordered all foreigners who had engaged in the opium trade to leave China. He was certain he had defeated the drug lords of Canton, and he wrote to the emperor to notify him of the victory. However, Lin was mistaken. Elliot secured safe passage for all the British merchants, and his agreement to hand over the opium didn't mean surrender

By June, all the British traders demanded China compensate them for their future losses since their government wouldn't. British Parliament approved the compensation of 2.5 million dollars to merchants who lost opium during their lockdown in Canton, but it refused to pay for any possible future losses, saying that was China's responsibility since they closed the market. However, China had no intention of giving any money for illegal drugs. Angered, a party of merchants called for British Parliament to send troops. Sir Charles Elliot joined them and asked for just enough troops to frighten the Chinese officials and urge them to return to the status quo.

But not everyone wanted the war. British merchants who traded in tea, silk, and porcelain greatly benefited from the discontinued illegal drug trade. A war would ruin their legitimate business and stop the trade in Chinese luxury goods. Christian missionaries were also celebrating the end of the opium imports, as they previously complained that a nation constantly high on drugs could not care about turning to Christ. A nation ravaged by war would think about conversion even less.

But Lin's confiscation of the opium in Canton was only one deed, and although it was dramatic enough to pause the drug trade, it wasn't enough to completely stop it. The headquarters of the drug lords was transferred to Macau, sixty miles south of Canton. Within just one month, the Chinese black market was once again flooded with opium. Instead of using Canton as an entry point, British opium traders sold in Macau, which was under Portuguese jurisdiction. It was on the Chinese buyers to smuggle it farther into China. The profits foreign merchants made skyrocketed, as Lin's efforts to ban opium only served as an excuse to increase the price.

However, on the outside, it seemed that Commissioner Lin Zexu managed to purify the country and get rid of not just the drug but also of foreign traders. Legal trade continued under the strict supervision of Chinese forces. Some of the British sailors in Kowloon (today a part of Hong Kong) got drunk and fought with a local villager. They beat him to death, and Elliot arrested them. He tried and sentenced them to six months of hard labor back in Britain. However, Lin Zexu wanted the perpetrators to be judged by Chinese laws. Elliot wouldn't comply with this, as he knew that the British sailors would be sentenced to death under Chinese law. This incident only served to raise tensions between Britain and China. The chief superintendent of trade wanted to settle the situation because the troops he demanded from Parliament were still on their way. He needed to buy time and avoid conflict with China until reinforcements arrived. So, Elliot invited Lin to send Chinese officials to observe the trial. But in Lin's opinion, Elliot was setting up an extrajudicial institution that rejected China's sovereignty.

Three days later, Commissioner Lin banned Chinese citizens from selling or supplying the British with food. To supervise the situation, Chinese warships entered Hong Kong Harbor. This instigated rumors that the Chinese commissioner was getting ready to invade Hong Kong, where the British merchants and Elliot were docked aboard their ships. In Macau, fearing the Chinese punishment, Portuguese Governor Don Adrião Acácio da Silveira Pinto ordered all British to leave. He didn't want his people to be punished for hiding the unwelcomed British. Within 24 hours, 250 British citizens boarded ships in the port of Macau, but bad weather kept them docked. The following day, on August 30th, the first reinforcements from India arrived. The gunboat *Volage* brought armaments and news of another warship coming soon, the *Hyacinth*.

Under the protection of the *Volage*, sixty ships carrying over two thousand British citizens, among them women and children, set sail from Macau to the Kowloon plateau, north of Hong Kong. At the time, Hong Kong wasn't a city but a set of small fishing villages, with a port large enough for the European ships to dock at. Running out of food, Elliot had to do something. He sent three ships, the *Louisa*, the *Volage*, and the *Pearl*, to buy food from the first village they encountered. However, Hong Kong Harbor was guarded by three Chinese warships. Instead of attacking, the British were ordered to try diplomacy first, and they asked for permission to buy food. The warships let them pass, but once on land, Chinese officials refused them to trade. They threatened their citizens with punishments if they traded with the British, and they even barred them inside the settlement to prevent them from trading.

Infuriated, Elliot sent an ultimatum to the imperial officials, stating that if they were not allowed to resupply, the British ships would start to fire. He set the deadline for 2 p.m. When he received no answer by 3 p.m., the British opened fire on the Chinese warships. The first to fire was Captain Henry Smith of the *Volage*. The First Opium War began on September 4th, 1839, with what is known in China as the Battle of Kowloon.

Even though the Chinese ships were much larger, they were equipped with updated cannons that aimed too high. They missed all three British ships. However, the *Louisa*, the *Volage*, and the *Pearl* ran out of ammunition quickly. The British ships were forced to retreat, and the Chinese pursued them. The wind died down, though, so the ships were unable to move farther. The first battle of the First Opium War ended in a stalemate. Exhausted, the Chinese warships returned to Hong Kong with the first wind, allowing the British to escape. China claimed victory, even though no damage or loss of life occurred on either side. Soon enough, they allowed the British to resupply, confident that the imperial government had the upper hand in the conflict.

Charles Elliot didn't want to continue the conflict without the approval of the British Parliament, but he couldn't stop what was about to happen in Macau. There, a British ship managed to sneak through the Portuguese watch and unload its opium cargo. Just as it left the harbor, a Spanish ship, the *Bilbaino*, docked. Chinese authorities confused the two ships and set the noncombatant *Bilbaino* ablaze as punishment for the unloaded opium. In response, Governor Pinto armed his Portuguese ships, but the Chinese retreated. Elliot was eager to help the Portuguese governor, but the governor declined, as the crisis was temporarily settled.

The battleship *Hyacinth* finally arrived in Hong Kong, but Elliot refused to enter into another battle against the Chinese. On both sides, passions had calmed, and the hostilities had dissipated. Lin Zexu didn't even insist on the surrender of sailors who were responsible for the deaths of Chinese villagers anymore. However, he did urge all foreigners to sign the document that promised they would not trade in opium under the threat of the death penalty. Elliot realized the only way to stop the conflict with China was to abolish the drug trade, but he was also aware that the high profits were too tempting. He knew British merchants would continue hauling opium from India, no matter what. Because of it, he refused to sign the document, and he banned all British merchants from signing it as well.

The independent British traders, whose businesses were legitimate and who never traded in opium, went behind Elliot's back to sign the document. After all, they were not in any danger. Captain Warner of the *Thomas Coutts*, who traded in cotton from Bombay's factories, was the first to sign. He secured a legal opinion in India that Elliot's band could not enforce British law. Soon, other British vessels followed the example of Captain Warner, and Commissioner Lin Zexu saw the crack in the British resilience. Again, he resumed his resolve to punish the murderers of Chinese villagers, threatening to expel all the British from China.

Elliot's hands were tied, but he did receive good news from London. A letter from Lord Palmerston, the British foreign secretary, arrived, in which he promised sixteen ships and 4,000 troops would arrive in China by the next summer. All Elliot needed to do was sit patiently and prolong the status quo between the two nations. However, pressed by the fact that many British ships had signed Lin's document, Elliot had to act. On November 2nd, 1839, Elliot ordered the British ships under his command to block the entrance of incoming British ships to the Pearl River and Canton. Unaware of what was going on, the *Royal Saxon*, carrying rice from Java, arrived at the Chinese coast. Afraid this British ship would disobey his ban on signing the document, Elliot ordered the captain of the *Volage* to fire.

Nearby were fifteen Chinese warships and fourteen fire ships, whose task was to protect the ships coming into the Chuenpi harbor. Seeing that the British fired upon an independent trader, the Chinese, under the command of Admiral Guan Tianpei, responded. They anchored their ships between the *Royal Saxon* and the British warships as protection.

The British fired first. Since their fleet was inferior, Admiral Guan couldn't do much. They had stationary guns that couldn't directly aim at the enemy; they could only shoot above them. The Chinese lost four warships before the First Battle of Chuenpi was finished. Realizing they had no chance against the superior British warships, they were forced to run. Elliot knew there was no point in pursuing them, as it would trap his ships in between the Chinese fleets. However, because the *Royal Saxon* was defended, the Chinese proclaimed victory, even though they didn't manage to damage a single British ship. The imperial fleet, consisting of twenty-nine ships, couldn't match the power of the two British warships, the *Volage* and the *Hyacinth*.

Chapter 3 – The First Conflicts

Charles Elliot, Chief Superintendent of Trade
(https://en.wikipedia.org/wiki/Charles_Elliot#/media/
File:Charles_Elliot.png)

Christened by the London *Times*, the First Opium War officially started with the naval battle at Chuenpi, even though the British government refused to admit the cause of the war was the illegal trade in opium. Some members of Parliament even stated that the drug was not as dangerous as the Chinese presented it and that they never heard of anyone having impaired health due to opium, not even the workers in the Indian factories who were exposed to it for most of the day. The British justified the war by saying the Chinese were trying to stop their imperial treasury from losing silver. They continued by saying how Imperial China didn't care about its people's health and that hypocrisy guided their actions.

In India, where opium was initially produced, the Chamber of Commerce of both Calcutta and Bombay complained to the British Crown, asking for the compensation promised by Elliot. They also urged the government to respond to Lin's confiscation of opium with military action. However, the people of Britain and the United State condemned the actions taken by the British overseas and took the side of China. They wanted the opium trade to stop, as they didn't want to engage in yet another war. To change public opinion, the British government started exaggerating the events of Canton, accusing Lin Zexu of instigating the massacre of foreigners. In reality, Lin only besieged the foreign quarter. But the government needed people to condemn his actions, so London newspapers started printing gruesome stories about the lives of the British citizens in Canton.

Just in time, the first merchants who had resided in Canton arrived back in London. With them, they brought stories of the terrible treatment they underwent during the Chinese siege. They were paid by the biggest opium sellers to publish such stories to lobby for war. William Jardine of Jardine, Matheson & Co., one of the largest opium traders, even admitted in a letter to his colleague Matheson that he hired journalists to help write false stories of Chinese cruelty.

However, there were plenty of traders who only dealt with legal merchandise, and they demanded the British Parliament to end opium trafficking. They had the support of Anglican missionaries, who wrote extensive reports on the drug's influence on Chinese society. People continued to condemn the drug and the British efforts to keep importing it to foreign lands. But Parliament and Lord

Palmerston remained unmoved by the pleas of the public. Unfortunately, profit was the only thing that mattered. Palmerston called the anti-opium lobbyists troublemakers and unemployed activists. But since Palmerston didn't want to be the one responsible for a war, he planned to do nothing and hope that the problem would go away on its own.

Angered by Palmerston's approach, the opium merchants were determined to change his mind. Among them was Charles Elliot, who sent letters from Canton blaming the Chinese for unjust violence. He further wrote that even though he was personally against the opium trade, all it would take to solve the China problem was to block the coast from Peking to Canton with British warships. Finally, Parliament was persuaded, and they wrote back to Elliot on February 20th, 1840, to prepare for war. Officially, the British were sending their navy to China not to fight for the right to sell opium but to protect their colony in Canton from the oppression of Chinese officials. Palmerston accused the Chinese government of trying to exterminate all the British traders, and he claimed the British had to defend their honor.

Lord Palmerston included in his letter to Elliot a list of objectives that he wanted the war with China to achieve. It was on Elliot to see that the letter reached the Daoguang Emperor himself for the negotiations between the two nations to begin. Among other things, the list included the demand that the British superintendent was allowed to execute justice upon the British citizens in China, gain compensation for all the lost British merchandise (including opium), the right for foreigners to own property in China, open more ports to the British merchants aside from Canton, and secure an island or several islands along the Chinese coast where the British would set up their base.

Back in China, Lin Zexu's efforts to stop the opium import brought him recognition and a promotion. He became the governor-general of Guangdong and Guangxi provinces. But his crusade against opium had only just started. With renewed vigor, he started learning everything he could about the foreigners. Lin believed that to fight the enemy, one had to know the enemy. He purchased the *Cambridge*, a British warship, and moored it at the Pearl River's mouth. Unfortunately, before selling the warship, the British took out all its cannons and shipped them back to India. Lin Zexu was left with nothing more but an empty husk of a ship. The Chinese crew of the newly bought vessel didn't know how to operate its sails, so the ship couldn't even be moved.

It didn't help that the Chinese officials, together with the Daoguang Emperor, believed they had successfully gotten rid of the British. The majority of merchants had left Canton, and only Captain Charles Elliot remained, waiting for reinforcements. But the Chinese believed the British threat had passed, and they focused on preparing for the Sino-Sikh War, which occurred the next year. Lin Zexu was alone in his efforts to guard the approach to Canton.

Elliot was impatient, so he decided to move things forward and map the Yangtze River for future attacks. For the mission, he borrowed the *Hellas*, an opium trading ship. This ship saw battle as early as May 22nd, 1840, while it was becalmed at Namoa. The ship found itself surrounded by what seemed like Chinese merchant ships. These Chinese vessels soon opened fire on the *Hellas*. They even attempted to board the British ship but to no avail. After four hours of battle, the wind picked up the sails of the British ship, allowing it to escape. Luckily, there were no casualties, and the crew safely retreated with minor injuries.

Encouraged by the victory at Namoa, the Chinese decided to send their fleet to attack the British ships docked at Capsingmun, east of Macau. They used fire barges, which were supposed to collide with the moored ships and cause explosions. However, the *Druid*, *Volage*, and *Hyacinth* were quick to react. They used towing hooks to move away from the burning barges and the docked British ships. That day, no vessel was lost.

The very next day, on June 9th, 1840, the military reinforcements Lord Palmerston had promised finally arrived. The East India Company sent four steamers equipped with guns: the *Atlanta*, *Enterprise*, *Madagascar*, and *Queen*. Britain sent also sent seventeen men-of-war and three battleships: the *Wellesley*, *Blenheim*, and *Melville*. Later, they were joined by another battleship, the *Nemesis*. But the British sent more than military help. The armada was accompanied by many civilian ships, which carried around 10,000 opium chests. They needed military protection to be able to approach China's coast and unload their merchandise. The arrival of the fleet meant the British government approved of the illegal opium trade, so foreign merchants felt encouraged to bring the drug to the shores of China once again. The result, however, was a sudden drop in opium prices because the market was oversaturated with the drug.

The gathering place for this fleet was Singapore. The Chinese ships could only watch from a safe distance offshore at the gathering of the mighty British navy. They were aware their antique battleships were no match for their enemy's modern navy. On June 1st, the first offensive from Singapore was launched. The first ship to reach Canton Bay was the *Madagascar*. Captain Elliot waited at Macau, where he boarded the *Wellesley* and met Commodore J. J. Gordon Bremer. Even though they had all the might of the British navy under their command, the captain and the commodore were to attempt every possible diplomatic approach to the China problem first. The role of the battleships was more to frighten the enemy than to fight them. They would only engage in battle if everything else failed.

But to gain the upper hand in the negotiations, the British had to at least partially block the Chinese coastline. While Elliot suggested blocking Shanghai, Admiral Sir John Barrow wanted to take Hong Kong and Canton Bay. After the arrival of Admiral Sir George Elliot, cousin of Captain Charles Elliot, the British decided to block Canton and wait for the monsoon season to end. However, the merchants were unsatisfied with this slow progress. They wanted a swift frontal attack that would unblock trade immediately. The orders from London, though, were to press the Chinese just enough to agree to negotiations. From there, the British navy was to continue with a small-scale offensive until the Chinese accepted all the terms of the peace treaty.

The fighting began on July 1ˢᵗ, 1840, when the British armada launched an attack on Dinghai, a city on Chusan (Zhoushan) Island. The plan was to take the whole Chusan Archipelago and make it a British base. The city was protected by a five-sided wall encircled with canals. Even though the city housed around 40,000 people, there were only around 600 defendants. The rest were fishermen and sailors. A militia of 600 men is not small, but they were only armed with bows and spears. The occasional antique matchlock was present, but the lack of training prevented the people from using them efficiently.

The British armada was followed by twelve Chinese warships, which kept the distance, as they were aware of how weak they were. Nevertheless, they sent an invitation to the British to talk to a government official who was stationed on their flagship. It turns out the Chinese official in question wasn't a high-ranking naval officer as Commodore Bremer had hoped. He was just a commander of a local garrison. Bremer demanded the total surrender of Chusan, but the Chinese chose to ignore him. Instead, they prepared for the upcoming attack. On July 5ᵗʰ, Bremer fired the first shot at the small fishing village, and once the Chinese responded with a single shot, he ordered the return of fire with all seventy-four guns stationed on the *Wellesley*. The landing party followed soon after, led by Lieutenant Colonel George Burrell, commander of the 18ᵗʰ Brigade. In the meantime, four Chinese warships were destroyed, while others were damaged. The towers of the fort near the village were also destroyed, together with the wall that faced the sea.

With the shore secured, the British were able to move to the city of Dinghai, which lay one mile inland and was protected by surrounding hills. But the Indian artillery climbed those hills and started firing on the people of Dinghai from above. The British suffered no casualties during the first invasion, while around 2,000 Chinese lost their lives. The first British territory on the Chinese coast was taken on July 6th, 1840. Lin Zexu tried to warn the governors of Jiangsu and Zhejiang provinces, to which the Chusan Archipelago belonged, but they ignored him. Once the Daoguang Emperor received the news, he took no other action but to blame Lin Zexu. Lin was simply a scapegoat who paid for the loss of Chusan, and he was exiled to Xinjiang, a northern province inhabited by the Muslim Uyghurs. Even though he was disgraced, Lin would recover and become the viceroy of Shaanxi-Gansu province. Condemned and blamed for starting the First Opium War, he would later become the symbol of the fight against opium during the Second Opium War.

Even though Admiral George Elliot banned opium ships from landing in Chusan, his orders were ignored. By November 1840, the island became the main point for unloading the drug, and the price reached its lowest point, selling for just $100 per chest. By the end of the year, forty-three opium ships were docked at Chusan, and around 12,000 chests of opium were unloaded. So, even though opium was banned, it overflowed the streets of the British settlement. There were so many addicts on Chusan Island that missionaries came to open an addiction treatment center. The British soldiers were employed to guard the center, but these were the same soldiers who defended the smugglers of the drug from the Chinese navy stationed nearby.

British soldiers were unaccustomed to the warm Chinese climate, and despite the heat, they were ordered to station at the rice fields instead of the abandoned houses of Dinghai, where they would have been more comfortable. Lieutenant Colonel Burrell even ordered them to keep their uniforms neatly fastened, placing his soldiers in even more discomfort. Soon, dysentery swept through the ranks, taking over 600 lives. Because of this, Burrell was fired and replaced by Hugh Gough. Once the *Blenheim* and *Wellesley* sailed into

Dinghai, the British had enough firepower to continue toward Peking (Beijing). But first, Captain Charles Elliot had to try to send Palmerstone's letter to the emperor. He gave it to Chinese officials stationed twenty miles northwest of Dinghai. The letter came back to him, unopened and without explanation.

The next opportunity to pass the letter presented itself after ten days, when the British fleet entered the Bei He River seventy-five miles south from Peking. There, the letter was received by the governor of Chihli (Zhili) province, who agreed to send it to the emperor. Now, Elliot just had to wait for the reply. While waiting, he and his men were treated as guests by the Chinese and were supplied with food and water. Unfortunately, the British crew was struck by dysentery again, and in an attempt to find a freshwater source, Elliot ordered the fleet to scatter. On July 27th, he received an invitation to meet a state official named Jing'an Qishan. The negotiations lasted for six hours, but no deals were made.

Chapter 4 – Steamships and Guns

The Nemesis *(right background), destroying Chinese war junks by Esward Duncan*

(https://en.wikipedia.org/wiki/First_Opium_War#/media/File:Destroying_Chinese_war_junks,_by_E._Duncan_(1843).jpg)

During the First Opium War, steam-powered ships made their debut in warfare. The *Nemesis*, which was built in 1839, arrived in China a year later on November 25th, 1840. It was the first ship of its kind to traverse such a route, and its captain was William Hall, the first British officer to study the power of steam engines. The *Nemesis* was a thing to admire, and the Chinese were genuinely intimidated by the powerful steamship, as it was something they had never seen before.

At the time of the *Nemesis*'s arrival, the second round of negotiations between the two Elliots and Jing'an Qishan occurred in Canton. This was where the British officials first heard that Lin Zexu had been removed from the position of governor, for Qishan was the one elevated to Lin's former position. This was great news for Charles Elliot, who knew Lin and his hatred for opium very well.

Encouraged by this turn of events, Elliot demanded the opening of four more ports to the British traders: Amoy, Ningbo, Shanghai, and Fuzhou. He also demanded an unspecified island on which the British could settle their base, reimbursement for all the opium confiscated by Lin Zexu, and reparations for the British efforts in China. Qishan agreed to pay reparations of six million dollars over twelve years, but the agreement on the cessation of Chinese territory was a more complicated matter. The Chinese officials refused to release any territory to the British, even though Elliot promised to release Chusan in exchange for another port that would be chosen at a later date. Qishan decided to ignore Elliot's demand, prolonging the negotiations. New Year's Eve of 1841 passed, and there was still no progress in the negotiations. The impatient Charles Elliot gave Qishan two days, after which, he promised, the war would resume.

On January 7th, 1841, at 8 a.m., the British and Indian navies attacked Chuenpi Fort and its twin across the Pearl River, Tycocktow Fort. The Chinese returned fire but quickly realized they could do nothing. After five minutes of returning fire, the forts went silent. The bombardment from the *Nemesis*, *Enterprise*, *Madagascar*, and *Hyacinth* continued, while two companies of marines landed and crossed the walls of Chuenpi Fort. They fought the 2,000 Qing elite troops, who would not surrender. Only after 600 Chinese soldiers died did the rest flee or surrender. The British lowered the Chinese yellow flag and raised the Union Jack. The fight was over by 11:30 a.m. The British had only thirty-eight casualties, and none of them were fatal.

The attack on Tycocktow Fort was led by the *Samarang*, *Druid*, *Modeste*, and *Columbine*. They bombarded the walls of the fort with such precision that the Chinese were quickly silenced. The crews of these British warships stormed Tycocktow Fort and drew the Chinese completely out of it. By 11:20, the fighting was over.

On the sea, the *Nemesis* and its retinue of British men-of-war sank eleven Chinese warships at the mouth of the Pearl River. The Chinese ships never even returned fire. The British slaughtered them nonetheless, and the Second Battle of Chuenpi was over in less than four hours. But the war wasn't. Another battle, this time a naval one, occurred at Ansons Bay to the east of Chuenpi. There, the *Nemesis* demonstrated its power and proved the steamship was a navy onto itself. It alone sank fifteen Chinese war junks. Realizing the power of this new technology, the remaining fourteen Chinese ships began to flee, but Nemesis didn't follow. Instead, the steamship's captain decided to move it upstream to rejoin the British fleet.

There were three more forts in close vicinity of Chuenpi Fort, and the British were just about to fire at them when they received a message from the leader of the Chinese troops, Admiral Guan, who demanded a three-day ceasefire to consult with Governor Qishan. Elliot agreed, and soon, the negotiations were resumed. By January 20th, 1841, the two officials came to an agreement known in history as the Convention of Chuenpi. However, both the Chinese and British governments rejected the terms on which Elliot and Qishan agreed. Instead, they chose to replace their representatives and try to parley once more. While Lord Palmerston believed that Britain gained too little, the Daoguang Emperor believed China was giving too much. Instead of Elliot and Qishan, Henry Pottinger and Yang Fang were chosen to renew the negotiations.

Among the terms to which Elliot and Qishan agreed was the sale of Hong Kong to the British at the price of six million dollars. It was the same amount the Chinese had to pay for the war indemnity. The deal would neutralize the Chinese loss, but both Lord Palmerston and the Daoguang Emperor were infuriated by it. Palmerston wanted all of his initial demands fulfilled, while Elliot believed the British government couldn't ask for more after the slaughter of Chinese soldiers. However, Palmerston needed money to compensate the merchants for their lost opium; otherwise, the British Parliament would fall. He needed Elliot to secure the payment for both the war indemnities and the confiscated opium. Elliot, with his anti-opium beliefs, didn't even bother to bring the subject of the drug trade up, which further angered Palmerston, who wanted opium to be seen as lawful commerce.

In Peking, the Daoguang Emperor was outraged that Qishan agreed to give away Hong Kong, a sovereign territory of the Qing Empire. He punished Qishan with imprisonment and treason charges. He was even sentenced to death, but after a few months, he was released and allowed to continue helping in the negotiations with Britain. Still believing that he was a celestial emperor, the Daoguang Emperor also dared to order Charles Elliot to report to Peking for execution. His order was ignored.

When Elliot and Qishan signed the Convention of Chuenpi on January 20th, the emperor sent military reinforcements to Canton, ordering Qishan to stop all negotiations and attack the British. However, the Chinese official decided to disobey his emperor, as he believed the convention was good for both sides. A new conflict escalated when Lieutenant Colonel Burrell occupied Hong Kong on January 26th. A month later, the Chinese reinforcements from inland arrived and started gathering around the Bocca Tigris (the Humen strait). Realizing that diplomacy had failed, Elliot ordered the *Melville*, *Queen*, *Wellesley*, and *Druid* to fire at the forts of Wangtong and Anunghoi. The Chinese returned fire but stopped after only fifteen minutes. British and Indian soldiers then stormed the shore. The

Chinese soldiers fled, leaving the civilians to be slaughtered by the British soldiers.

A few days later, Elliot, who was on board the *Nemesis*, moved the fleet toward Canton, whose citizens fled. The deserted city was now occupied by the British. Elliot blamed the opium trade for the war, and he banned it from Canton. However, he removed the death penalty for the traders who were caught smuggling the drug. Instead, their contraband would be confiscated, but they would not be punished. Chinese General Yang Fang asked for a truce, and Elliot agreed. But the Chinese continued to gather their troops outside of Canton and even set up a price for the capture of the British. Elliot's head was estimated to be worth around 50,000 dollars.

General Yang Fang was tasked to retrieve Hong Kong from British hands. He was a veteran of the Chinese army, and at the age of seventy, he was already completely deaf. He had to write the orders for his soldiers. However, he still inspired awe among the troops and had great authority over them. He was no diplomat, though, and he believed that the end of the problems with the British would be to allow the opium trade to resume. The emperor disagreed and urged him to return with Elliot to the negotiating table.

On May 21ˢᵗ, 1841, the Chinese bombarded the foreign quarter of Canton. Luckily, Elliot ordered all the citizens to evacuate the city the day before, and no one was there except for a few stubborn merchants. Once again, the *Nemesis* proved its worth. While other British warships were becalmed, the steamship was able to move to safety, silencing the artillery from the Chinese forts and winning the naval battle by the next morning. Thus, the Chinese failed to force the British fleet to retreat. On May 27ᵗʰ, the negotiations continued, albeit briefly. General Fang wasn't satisfied with the progress of the parley, and he decided to attack Canton again. The Chinese forces managed to invade the city, enter the foreign quarter, and loot them. Elliot bombarded the city from *Nemesis*, with other British warships helping this time, but he decided against invading the city because his forces had been decimated by dysentery. While the Chinese had managed to gather around 20,000 soldiers, Elliot was down to around only 200. Close combat would be a suicide mission for the British.

A new treaty was signed on May 29th, 1841, which reimbursed the British with six million dollars. Other terms upon which the officials of the two nations agreed were the demilitarization of Canton and reimbursement to the Spanish, whose *Bilbaino* had been mistakenly destroyed by the Chinese two years earlier. Hong Kong, opium, and the resumption of trade were not even mentioned because both sides wanted to stop the fighting immediately. The British officials agreed they would not demand the Chinese to admit defeat in order to save the emperor's face and convince him to agree to the terms.

This treaty, known as the "Ransom of Canton," resulted in the British retreating to Hong Kong. The Chinese painted a picture of victory, describing the British as barbarians who begged for mercy, money, and the resumption of trade. The Daoguang Emperor was never informed that the British fleet had not been destroyed and that it had safely retreated to Hong Kong. He was led to believe their victory was complete, so he demanded Hong Kong back. General Yang Fang was criticized for letting the British go and for not pursuing them. The inaccurate reports that were sent to the emperor would have disastrous effects.

Since the opium trade problem was still not solved, British Parliament decided the war must continue. This time, they decided that Peking (Beijing) must be pressured and that the army must move north. The first target of the renewed conflict was the city of Amoy (Xiamen), whose fall would block the Yangtze River. But while preparing for the expedition, a typhoon hit Hong Kong, damaging the British fleet. It was then Elliot found out that he had been fired from the position of chief superintendent of trade. He wasn't notified through any official means of communication. Instead, he had found out from the *Canton Press*, an English newspaper published in Canton.

Back in Britain, Charles Elliot had been presented in the press as the weakling who made peace with the inferior Chinese instead of achieving a decisive victory. The stories about the ex-superintendent made him a villain in the eyes of the public. Palmerston accused him of ignoring direct orders and acting without the approval of the British navy or government. Aside from being a traitor, he was also accused of softness toward the enemy and a love for the Chinese. Elliot was to be replaced by Henry Pottinger, while the command of the land troops in China remained in the hands of Sir Hugh Gough.

Pottinger could be described as a Sinophobe, as he had little to no understanding of the Chinese culture and protocols. Nevertheless, he was greeted with all the honors on his arrival. No one escorted Elliot and his family on their way back to Britain.

The British gathered a new armada, consisting of thirty-two ships, four of which were steamers carrying 27,000 men. On August 21st, the armada left Macau and started toward Amoy. The importance of Amoy lay in its proximity to Peking. It was a barren island 300 miles north of Macau, and the British reached it in four days. The citadel on the island was equipped with 200 guns and 96 embrasures, through which the Chinese soldiers shot their arrows and matchlocks. An additional forty-two guns were added once the Chinese heard of the British plan to attack Amoy. Kulangsu Island, which acted as protection to Amoy, also had a citadel equipped with seventy-six guns. The rare modern artillery was stationed here, but it didn't help. The *Modeste*, *Blonde*, and *Druid* bombarded the walls of Kulangsu's citadel and brought it down quickly.

Amoy was bombarded for ninety minutes. The antique Chinese guns were stationary, so they couldn't aim at the British armada. Instead, they shot too high, missing all the enemy ships. Soon, they fell silent. The British soldiers disembarked, and Sir Hugh Gough led the charge, attacking the Amoy fort from the south. The Chinese tried to defend the citadel but had to retreat, carrying their wounded with them. Realizing the battle was lost, the Manchu commander committed suicide. Among other personal items the Chinese soldiers left behind at the citadel, the British found opium pipes. The imperial defenders of Amoy were intoxicated by the very drug they were fighting against.

The British spent a week in Amoy, where they set up a garrison. The looting of civilian houses was strictly forbidden, and Gough had to execute several of his men for disobeying this order. Once the garrison was raised, and the storms passed, the British were ready to move toward Peking. Admiral Sir William Parker and Henry Pottinger decided to take the fort of Dinghai on Chusan Island. The Chinese put up an impressive fight, but they were still no match for the modernized British navy.

The British wanted to capture the whole central coast of China, and their next target was the city of Jinhai. On October 10th, the attack began. However, Jinhai had better defenses. The fort rested on a cliff and had 4,000 Chinese troops defending it. Being ten miles away from the shore, the success of an attack on this city depended on the forces of General Gough. He took 1,500 men and flanked the fort. In less than twenty-four hours, the British declared victory. The British suffered only three casualties, while several hundred Chinese died defending the city. Three days later, when the British armada approached Ningbo, the city opened its gates, surrendering without a fight. The British army settled there for the winter.

At the end of 1841, the Daoguang Emperor finally learned that his state officials were sending him false information about events in Canton and that he had claimed victory when there was none. Angered, he sent his cousin Yijing to retrieve Ningbo. But Yijing's army was ill-trained and consisted mostly of villagers he recruited en route to Soochow, fifty miles north from Ningbo. He still managed to gather 5,000 people, and on March 10th, 1842, he led the attack on British-occupied Ningbo. The Chinese soldiers were under the influence of opium, which diminished their fighting skills, and aside from their numbers, they were in no position to fight the militarily superior British. A mere 150 men under the command of General Gough managed to repel Yijing's attack.

The effects of Ningbo's loss were devastating for Chinese morale. Many soldiers deserted, and the Imperial Army was decimated. The Chinese didn't believe the war against the British was worth fighting, especially with the majority of the population being addicted to opium anyways. Even high-ranking military officials were often found dead on the battlefield with opium pipes in their hands. The small conflicts that occurred during the spring of 1842 often saw Chinese soldiers running through the battlefields while dazed by opium. The result of the demilitarization of Canton and the British takeover of Hong Kong resulted in increased opium trade. The market was again oversaturated with the drug, but it never lacked addicts willing to buy it. The same soldiers who fought the British were helping the opium traders unload their cargo in the available Chinese ports.

British-owned Hong Kong went through a metamorphosis during this period. From scattered small fishing villages, it grew into a modern Westernized city. By February 1842, the city was swarmed with builders and various workers who updated and built it to British standards. The drug trade flourished here. It is estimated that 25 percent of the ships carrying opium unloaded their contraband in Hong Kong, where it then found its way to mainland China.

Back in Britain, a governmental change occurred. The dissatisfaction with the outcome of the war with China was one of the reasons, but it was also impacted by the downfall of Prime Minister Lord Melbourne and his Whig Parliament. They were replaced by the Tories and Sir Robert Peel, who had strongly advocated against the war. However, once in power, they did nothing to stop it. They were actually accused of escalating the conflict. They sent 100 ships and the whole 5ᵗʰ Regiment to China to help Gough, whose troop numbers increased from 3,000 to 10,000. The hostilities were resumed in June 1842.

Chapter 5 – The End of the First Opium War

Sir Henry Pottinger

On June 16th, 1842, at the mouth of the Yangtze River, the next attack occurred. The plan was to gain control of the river and cut off the strategically important city of Nanjing (Nanking), which was 175 miles inland. The city was a metropolis, and the British hoped its fall would persuade the emperor to sit at the negotiating table. The other plan was to attack the capital itself, but the British wanted to avoid doing so at all costs. But before Nanjing, they had to deal with Shanghai. Shanghai surrendered without a fight, and during the week they spent there, the British soldiers looted and raped. One of the Chinese officials who lived there wrote in his memoirs how the enemy was satisfied with looting and left the city without slaughtering its people.

The next target was the city of Zhenjiang. The British soldiers who were tasked with capturing this city suffered dehydration, and twenty of them died. They were the only casualties of this battle, even though the Chinese defenders poured fire down on the British soldiers. After the city was taken, the British generals agreed that their reputation as looters and rapists had to stop. They arrested and hanged all of their soldiers who indulged in rape. British generals showed their racist tendencies by accusing and punishing only Indians, which suggests they might have been scapegoats. Nevertheless, they served as a warning to other soldiers.

Racial differences surfaced among the Chinese ranks too. The Manchus, the ruling elite, considered themselves superior to Chinese. Manchu General Hailin blamed the Chinese citizens for conspiring with the enemy, and he rounded them up and executed them, even though they were innocent civilians. The Chinese feared the British just as much as they feared their Manchu masters. Hailin spared no one, and he even rewarded his soldiers for killing "traitorous" women and children.

With the capture of Zhenjiang, the British controlled all the traffic on the Yangtze River, be it commercial or military. The salt and grain transportation to Nanjing was cut off, as well as the communication of Chinese merchants. Nanjing, the former capital of the Ming dynasty, was now completely exposed to the British. The Daoguang Emperor was forced to act and seek peace. If the enemy took strategically important Nanjing, there was nothing to stop them from advancing to Peking, where the Son of Heaven resided.

Yilibu, Viceroy of Nanjing, and Qiying, a Manchu official, was appointed as plenipotentiaries by the emperor himself. As such, they had the power to lead and conclude the peace treaty with the British. The Daoguang Emperor ordered them to accept any terms that would stop the British advancement toward the capital. However, the newly appointed diplomats hesitated with the negotiations, as they didn't want to bring down the emperor's wrath upon themselves. To persuade them to parley, Sir Henry Pottinger threatened the bombardment of Nanjing's city walls. After two days with no answer, the *Cornwallis* was brought within firing range of the city to support the threat. However, Pottinger still didn't order the attack. Finally, Yilibu agreed to read the British peace treaty proposal, even though he still declined to see Henry Pottinger in person.

Yilibu resorted to the old Chinese tactic of passive procrastination to buy himself some time. Even after ten days, Pottinger had not received an answer. Finally, he set the date of August 13th as the day when the attack on Nanjing would begin. As a result, Yilibu swallowed his pride and agreed to board the *Queen*, see Pottinger in person, and start the parley. After four days, Yilibu accepted the British terms for peace, but despite having all the power to sign the document himself, he insisted on the emperor's approval. He was afraid of the death sentence in case the treaty displeased the ruler. Because of it, Yilibu renounced his plenipotentiary power, forcing the British to wait for an answer from Peking.

While waiting for the emperor's response, Yilibu continued the talks with Pottinger, and what will become known as the Treaty of Nanjing slowly took form. The Chinese official realized that the opium trade was in the middle of it, and he refused to discuss it at the beginning. The stubborn Pottinger insisted, and all Yilibu could do was agree to drop the matter, which would allow the illegal trade to continue even though he detested the drug. The terms the Chinese diplomat accepted were humiliating and disgraceful. The reparation cost was raised from six million to twenty-one million dollars. He also accepted the British demand for access to the port of Fuzhou. Yilibu accepted all the peace terms the British demanded except for the legalization of the opium trade. Even though Pottinger was instructed to convince the Chinese that they could benefit from the trade by collecting taxes on the drug, he did not want to press the matter once he received a letter from the emperor himself. In the letter, the emperor said he would never resort to gaining profit off the misery of his people.

Sir Henry Pottinger realized China would never publicly admit the trade of opium. Therefore, he proposed a secret meeting that Chinese officials could later deny even happened. Yilibu agreed to this meeting, confirming that, for China, it was all about honor, not the good of the people. During the secret meeting, the Chinese officials asked Britain why they couldn't just stop producing opium in their Indian factories. They couldn't understand how the British Parliament had no power to halt the cultivation of poppies. All they ever knew was the totalitarian power of the emperor, and they couldn't understand the subtle politics of foreigners. Lord Pottinger defended Britain, saying the problem lay with the consumers, not the producers, and that the trade would stop if there wasn't any demand. He also defended the opium trade by saying that if it wasn't the British who sold it, then some other country, such as America or France, would jump on the opportunity to import the drug. After notifying the emperor about everything that happened during the meeting, Yilibu accepted all the terms of the treaty except the official acceptance of the opium trade. The document was signed on August 29th, 1842. It was ratified by the Daoguang Emperor on October 27th and by Queen Victoria on December 28th.

The final form of the treaty included three major points for the British: the changes to the Chinese approach to foreign trade, the cessation of Hong Kong, and reparations for the war. The monopoly on foreign trade was over, and four additional ports were opened to the British merchants: Amoy, Fuzhou, Ningbo, and Shanghai. The Chinese government had to pay six million dollars for the opium confiscated by Lin Zexu, three million dollars the Hong Kong merchants owed to the British, and another twelve million for war reparations. The total sum of twenty-one million dollars had to be paid over the next three years, with an interest rate of 5 percent if the money was not paid in time. Hong Kong became a British colony for an indefinite term. However, there would be several more conventions that determined the fate of Hong Kong. The last one occurred in 1997 when Hong Kong was transferred to China, but it still remained a special administrative region with its own politics and constitution.

With the end of the war and the Treaty of Nanjing, the Chinese were left angry and humiliated. This anger accumulated and eventually needed to be vented. An opportunity arose when the opium traders decided to enter Canton with their wives. The Chinese regarded this as breaking the tradition that demanded the sexes should not be mixed. In November 1884, the residents of Canton rioted, burning the British flag. The Americans who were defending the foreign quarter shot five rioters, while the Chinese police dispersed the crowd gathered there. Unable to express their anger on the foreign quarter, the rioters turned to two British ships docked at Canton, the *Ann* and the *Nerbudda*. The crew and the passengers of these ships were beheaded, except for a few who were spared to bring the message back to London. Pottinger threatened retaliation, but the viceroy of Canton quickly arrested all the rebel leaders.

Back in London, the Treaty of Nanjing was hailed as a victory. *The Illustrated London News* wrote that the Chinese war secured the flow of millions of dollars to the British and the continuation of the tea supply. The British newspapers celebrated the victory and never even mentioned the loss of lives, the hardship of the war, or even the illegal opium trade, the real cause of the war. Under the Crown's rule, Hong Kong became an important port, as all incoming opium was unloaded there. The Crown even offered protection for the buyers, and the number of residents in the new port increased exponentially. Opium remained the most sought-after contraband in China, and the supply continued to meet the demand.

Not everyone celebrated the victory over addiction-ravaged China. The London *Times* consistently condoned the opium trade, and after the Treaty of Nanjing, it wrote several articles condemning the war and the way British soldiers had behaved toward the locals and their culture. The Tory Party, which now ruled the British Parliament, consisted of Anglican members who continued to advocate against the opium trade. Foreign Secretary of State Lord Aberdeen said the British smugglers of opium must not receive any protection if they were to face the repercussions for breaking the law. Lord Pottinger was empowered to punish the drug dealing in Hong Kong, and he made it known that any British citizen caught smuggling opium by Imperial China would not have British support or protection.

Still, the opium trade continued to prosper in China, as the demand was so high. Some of the British officials supported and even encouraged it. The governor-general of India scolded the foreign secretary for his opinion on the opium trade. He believed the revenues this drug brought to Britain was far too great and shouldn't be interfered with. Lord Aberdeen had no support in his efforts to stop the opium trade, not even from the Tory prime minister. Eventually, he was bullied into submitting to the general opinion that the drug export to China was vital for the welfare of Britain.

The controversy over opium didn't end with the war. Prime Minister Sir Robert Peel pushed for the total legalization of opium. His spokesman, W. B. Baring, even addressed Parliament, saying the Chinese emperor did nothing to stop the opium trade; therefore, it must be legalized. It seems as if they forgot that Lin Zexu had successfully banned opium and stopped its trafficking through the confiscation of the drug. The opium trade had successfully stopped for four months due to the efforts of Lin Zexu.

To end the debate about the righteousness of the war and opium trade, Sir Robert Peel declared that the Chinese emperor agreed with the opium legalization and the British importation of the drug to China. This was a lie, served to shut down the debate and nothing else. He needed to save Parliament from falling apart, as the members couldn't agree. Although it was only temporary, Parliament was silenced on the topic of China, opium, and the war.

Sir Henry Pottinger was rewarded for his service during the First Opium War, and he became the governor of Madras and earned a pension of 1,500 pounds per year. Even though he was a plenipotentiary, he didn't receive the usual prize money for his successful diplomatic service. As for Sir Charles Elliot, he was punished for his failure to deal with the opium matter as ordered by Lord Palmerston. He was appointed as the governor of troublesome Bermuda, Trinidad, and finally St. Helena, where Napoleon was exiled.

In China, the emperor's anger over the humiliating Treaty of Nanjing made him punish Yilibu, who was sent to live in exile, chained like a common criminal. Qiying remained in the emperor's favor, and the emperor even forgave Lin Zexu, who was called back to serve as the viceroy of Shaanxi-Gansu province in 1845. However, five years later, Lin died while on his way to deal with the Taiping Rebellion, which occurred in Guangxi.

Chapter 6 – The Interwar Period

A photograph of two Chinese coolies
(https://en.wikipedia.org/wiki/Coolie#/media/
File:CHINESE_COOLIES.jpg)

Although the Treaty of Nanjing ended the First Opium War, the conflicts between China and Britain continued. The Treaty of Nanjing never mentioned opium, so the drug remained officially illegal in China. Unofficially, it continued to be a huge business, and both Britain and corrupt Chinese officials prospered. Eventually, opium would be the spark that would ignite yet another war. But the interval between the First and Second Opium Wars lasted for fourteen years, and it was what many historians today refer to as an armed truce. Newly opened ports at Shanghai and Amoy opened interior China to the opium trade, as smugglers started using the Yangtze River. Together with the Pearl River, Yangtze became a highway for the opium trade.

Although the British textile industry magnates dreamed about an open Chinese market for their cotton, they never managed to fully take over China. China had its own textile industry, which was capable of sustaining the whole nation. English cotton didn't successfully enter the market in China, as it was regarded as inferior. But Britain still remained one of the biggest consumers of Chinese tea and silk, and opium remained the only product Britain could sell in China. And it still wasn't enough to balance out the trade. While Britain spent around fifteen million dollars annually for tea and silk, China lost only seven million dollars on buying opium from the British colonies.

But silk, tea, and opium were not the only trade items exchanged between the Asian empire and the Western world. Even before all the hassle with opium, China was exporting its workers, known as coolies (slang for unskilled workers), who worked on the plantations of the American, Peruvian, British, French, and Portuguese colonies. The first coolies left China as early as 1806, hoping to find a better life in British-owned Trinidad and Jamaica. However, after the First Opium War, the labor export transformed into drugging and kidnapping Chinese people of lower social status and practically selling them into slavery.

While half of the coolies were volunteers who were promised better lives in foreign lands, the other half were people taken against their will. Both volunteers and the abducted people were confined into very small barracks where they lived no better conditions than pigs. They were even branded across their chests or backs with capital letters, such as P, A, or S, depending on where their destination was: P for Peru, A for America, or S for the Sandwich Islands. This is why the coolie trade was baptized as the "Pig Trade." Once they were ready to be shipped, the coolie-slaves were crammed up to 500 per one boat. They had no room to lie down and had to spend the whole journey across the Pacific on their feet. Up to 40 percent of them died during the journey, but the "Pig Trade" still brought enough profit to the slavers, for it seems that selling just 60 percent of their cargo was worthwhile. The Portuguese even declared the only profitable business at the time was the "Pig Trade."

Coolies weren't only Chinese. The practice started in India, where the unskilled workers of lower castes, especially the Kuli caste (which gave the name to the term coolie), were promised high wages in the overseas British colonies. The promise was one of deception, but Indians were always volunteers. There was no kidnapping and capturing of Indians, and they were even allowed to bring their women and children. The Chinese coolies, on the other hand, were male workers 99 percent of the time, and they were either tricked into slavery or taken against their will. There were some cases where women were kidnapped and sold to the plantation owners as sex slaves, but their demand was low. The usual contract the coolies signed with the coolies was for up to five to seven years. However, the workers needed to pay for the ship transport, and the price was so high that even after the end of the contract, they had to remain working on the plantations to pay off their debts. The conditions on the plantations and in the Peruvian silver mines were horrid. Seventy percent of coolies died before the end of their contract period, while the rest never managed to gather enough money to pay their debt, let alone return home. There is not one recorded case of a Chinese coolie returning home.

The slave trade was outlawed in 1807 in Britain, but this didn't stop the British merchants from profiting off of the "Pig Trade." It was the British who came up with the term "shanghaied" to describe the practice of kidnapping or tricking a person into slavery. After all, the British ports in China were the main hubs for human trafficking. Shanghai and Amoy housed the barracks in which the coolies were kept before they were shipped off. The British representatives in China did not turn a blind eye to the trade of the coolie-slaves. In 1852, a British official in Canton wrote to the foreign secretary in London, Lord Malmesbury, describing the horrors of human trafficking and rightfully comparing it to the one happening on the African continent.

Even the opium merchants were shocked and appalled by the "Pig Trade," and they sent their complaints to Parliament. It was the one thing that managed to unite the British Parliament and the public. Britain officially condemned the kidnapping and trade of coolies, even though many of its citizens took part in it. In 1855, the Chinese Passenger Act was passed in the United States of America, and Britain made sure this act was followed in their Chinese ports. This wasn't an official ban on human trafficking, but the conditions of human transport over the Pacific were significantly improved. The act regulated the living quarters for the passengers, including how tight the living quarters could be, the ventilation, cooking area, hospitals, and even the designs of the hatches and doors.

The Daoguang Emperor died in 1850, and in his will, he apologized to the people of China for accepting the humiliating Treaty of Nanjing. He was succeeded by his fourth son, who became known as the Xianfeng Emperor. He cared little for politics and spent most of his time in his concubine's bed in an opium daze. After giving him a son, this concubine was elevated to the position of empress, even though the Xianfeng Emperor was already married to a Manchu princess. Nevertheless, his love for the concubine was such that he named her the "Empress of the Western Palace," while his official wife was the "Empress of the Eastern Palace." This concubine was the famous Empress Cixi, who soon wielded enormous influence in the imperial court. After the death of the Xianfeng Emperor, she had enough support to stage a coup and overthrow the regency council. Together with the Empress of the Eastern Palace, she ruled China, first as a co-regent to her son, and then as the dowager empress once her son was old enough to ascend the throne. She ruled until she died in 1908.

Cixi herself was an opium addict, but she kept herself on maintained doses so she could function and wield control over the government. She had a pivotal role in many events that occurred during the Second Opium War, although, at the time, she was still just a concubine. As a highly educated woman, which was unusual for a Chinese female at the time, the emperor allowed her to read all the court manifestos and documents concerning politics. Cixi became an expert in the matters of the government, and since she was the Xianfeng Emperor's favorite concubine, she had an enormous influence on him.

During the reign of the Xianfeng Emperor, there was a drastic fall in the quality of Chinese bureaucracy. Previous generations of rulers allowed only a few of the high-class people to pass the rigorous imperial exams and become state officials. But the lack of silver in the royal treasury urged the Xianfeng Emperor to sell government offices to anyone who could afford it. Anyone in the middle class of society who had 800 pounds could enter the government service even without the necessary education. This opened the Chinese bureaucracy to even more corruption and incompetence.

This incompetence displayed itself the most during the famine that occurred in 1856 when Huang He (Yellow) River flooded and destroyed rice fields, which fed the capital and its Hebei province. Since the government failed to provide for its people during the famine, naturally, a rebellion followed. This rebellion, known as the Taiping Rebellion, had started in 1851 in Guangxi province after

Chinese officials started persecuting the God Worshiping Society, which fused Christianity with Daoism, Confucianism, and millenarianism. The rebellion eventually became an anti-Manchu movement that sought to bring the Qing dynasty down. The Taiping Rebellion combined the religious, anti-governmental, and starvation sentiments of the people into a civil war, which has an estimated casualty number between twenty and thirty million people. However, the Second Opium War was fought parallel with it, and it is impossible to distinguish the victims of the war and the rebellion with any certainty. The Taiping Rebellion ended in 1864, four years after the end of the Second Opium War.

The Qing dynasty was already weakened by the First Opium War. Famine followed, and the incompetent government didn't know what to do or how to deal with the civil uprising. The emperor allowed it to grow from a religious rebellion to a nationwide civil war that affected the whole empire. This was the prelude to the fall of the Qing dynasty, which never managed to recover. In less than fifty years after the end of the rebellion, another revolution would manage to bring the dynasty down.

Chapter 7 – Conflict on the Horizon

Earl James Bruce Elgin by Felice Beato
(https://en.wikipedia.org/wiki/James_Bruce,_8th_Earl_of_Elgin#/
media/File:Felice_Beato_(British,_born_Italy_-_Portrait_of_Lord
_Elgin,_Plenipotentiary_and_Ambassador,_Who_Signed
_the_Treaty_-_Google_Art_Project.jpg)

The first problem that sparked the Second Opium War occurred in October 1856 with the Arrow incident. A British ship named the *Arrow* had a troubling past. Built by the Chinese as a cargo ship, the *Arrow* was captured by pirates. Later, it was recaptured by the Chinese, who sold it to a merchant who worked for the British East India Company. The merchant used this connection to register the ship, making it officially British. However, he failed to purge the former crew, which included two pirates.

On the day of the incident, its Belfast captain, Thomas Kennedy, left his post to visit a friend, Captain John Leach. While Kennedy was chatting with Leach on another ship, two imperial junks approached the *Arrow*, which was docked at Canton, and started arresting its crew, who were all native Chinese. Once Kennedy managed to return to his ship, the Chinese officials refused to give him an explanation regarding the arrests but allowed him to keep two of his crew members as a skeleton crew. Kennedy was confused. To him, there was no logic in the actions of the Chinese officials. The *Arrow* was a cargo ship that transported rice, not opium, from Macau. It was later that he learned of the ship's past as a pirate vessel. The Chinese claimed they believed the ship was again serving the pirates, as its British registration had lapsed.

Kennedy reported the seizure of his crew to Harry Parkes, the British consul in Canton, who immediately complained directly to the officials on board the imperial junks. He demanded all twelve members of the *Arrow*'s crew to be released, and he cited the Supplementary Treaty of 1843, which required the Chinese to ask the British consul for permission to arrest Chinese citizens who served on British vessels. The imperial officials still refused to release the crew, saying that at least one of its members was a pirate and that they needed the rest to testify his guilt or innocence. Parkes wouldn't let the matter go. He was so demanding that one of the Chinese officials slapped him.

Humiliated, Parkes left the imperial junk and wrote a letter to Ye Mingchen, the imperial commissioner for foreign affairs and the viceroy of Guangxi and Guangdong provinces. But Ye was known for his brutality, which he used to crush the Taiping Rebellion in his two provinces. (Canton alone saw the execution of over 200 rebels and their families on more than one occasion when Ye was the governor of the city.) Ye replied that he could agree to release nine crewmen but that he had to keep the other three, claiming they were pirates. He also reminded Parkes that the *Arrow* was Chinese property since its British registration had expired, but in goodwill, he would send the nine crew members together with the letter.

After consulting with the governor of Hong Kong, Sir John Bowring, Parkes decided not to accept the nine crew members and instead wanted to pursue the question of the *Arrow* incident, as it may bring other diplomatic advantages for the British, such as permission to buy and own property in Canton outside of the foreign quarter. He planned to retaliate for the incident by seizing one of the Chinese war junks that were involved in the arrest of the *Arrow*'s crew. On October 14th, the British gunboat *Coramandel* boarded the Chinese ship and, after seizing it, towed it to Whampoa. However, Parkes failed to provoke the Chinese, as the vessel he seized was private property and not owned by the government. Therefore, Ye decided to ignore the incident. Since Parkes didn't agitate the Chinese official, Bowring decided to write a letter to Ye, in which he threatened that if all twelve prisoners were not released in the next twenty-four hours, the British naval officers would have to use force to push the Chinese into obedience. He also demanded an official apology from the viceroy.

Ye Mingchen remembered the horrors of the First Opium War, and he knew the British had a reputation of backing up their threats. He agreed to release the prisoners, but since honor was sacred in Chinese culture, he refused to apologize. He also stated that, in the future, the British consul would be contacted before Chinese authorities arrest any suspicious crew member on board British vessels. However, he asked Bowring not to issue the Hong Kong registry to the Chinese vessels to avoid future mistakes from occurring.

This reply wasn't enough for Parkes and Bowring, and they saw it as an excuse to launch an attack. On October 23rd, 1856, Admiral Sir Michael Seymour received the order to destroy the four Barrier Forts, which were stationed just south of Canton. Five defenders were killed in the attack before the forts were taken, and they are counted as the first casualties of the Second Opium War, also known as the Arrow War.

Next, Parkes threatened he would destroy Ye's residency, which was close to the water in Canton, if he didn't allow foreigners to reside outside of the foreign quarter. But the Chinese government defended the existence of the foreign quarter, saying that confining non-Chinese was for their protection. They claimed the Chinese were not used to foreigners living among them and that they would feel unwelcomed. In reality, they wanted the foreigners confined so they didn't spread their influence upon the Chinese citizens. After Ye refused to meet Parkes's demands, the British steamer *Encounter* bombarded the viceroy's residence.

All the British managed to achieve was to anger Viceroy Ye Mingchen, who called on the Chinese people to kill any foreigner they saw, outside or inside the city of Canton. He even offered a reward for each British head: one hundred dollars. Parkes's price was 30,000 dollars, while other high-ranking British were priced at 5,000.

The next day, the British blew a hole in Canton's wall and invaded the city. The Chinese guns on the walls never even returned fire. Although the conflict started between Britain and China, the US envoy to Hong Kong, James Keenan, planted the Stars and Stripes on top of the city wall, as well as on the rooftop of Viceroy Ye's residency. Up until now, America had remained neutral, and the actions of Keenan were seen as a result of his intoxication.

Once the British stormed the city, they attacked the viceroy's residency. No one was there to defend it, and the Chinese official fled the city, leaving it at the mercy of the British. However, Admiral Seymour didn't have enough men to hold the city, and he had to retreat to the safety of the camp outside its walls. Ye Mingchen sent emissaries, who were tasked with negotiating the peace with Parkes, but the consul refused peace. Instead, he threatened the British naval force would help the Taiping rebels. This was an empty threat, though, as he had no power or permission to do such a thing. But Seymour continued to bombard the city, forcing the residents, both Chinese and foreigners, to abandon Canton in fear for their lives.

Ye finally agreed to parley with the British, but he still considered it to be below his honor to meet them in person. Instead, he sent one of his subordinates. When Bowring demanded a personal meeting with Ye, the viceroy of Canton showed his defiance. He confirmed the bounty on the British heads and asked his people to hunt the foreigners and bring them to him, dead or alive. Seymour continued the siege of Canton, which stopped all trade. The Cohong merchants faced their doom, and on November 12th, they requested to see Parkes. The consul, however, decided there was nothing to be done to help the return of trade, as the Cohong merchants were not able to support British demands to reside outside the foreign quarter.

The Taiping rebels hoped they would gain British support since they had a common enemy: the Chinese emperor. However, the British were reluctant to ally with the rebels, mostly because of their religious views. When the rebel armada of around fifteen ships tried to enter Canton Harbor and offer their help in taking the city, the British refused and escorted them away. However, Harry Parkes used the Taiping offer of help to intimidate Ye, saying that they refused the rebels for now, but the decision could always be changed. The British even refused the offer of some 200 Chinese commoners who offered to fight on the British side. They were afraid of treason, and they simply couldn't trust any Chinese.

On December 14th, Ye ordered the destruction of the foreign quarter in Canton, although he denied being involved at all. A procession of Chinese, who bore torches, entered the foreign quarter and set all the buildings ablaze. Unfortunately, the foreigners who decided to return were unable to extinguish the flames. One British citizen lost his life due to the fire, and the only building that remained was the British chapel. It is possible the viceroy's bounty on British heads was responsible for the blaze, as well as for other violent incidents occurring around the city. For example, the Chinese crew of the steamship *Thistle*, which carried mail, raised a mutiny, in which they killed all the European passengers. The ship was then set ablaze and left to drift toward Canton, with the bodies of the victims in the ship's bowels. They were all missing heads, as the Chinese needed them to collect the bounty.

Another incident occurred in Hong Kong. There, all the foreigners got their bread from the same baker. On January 15th, 1857, all of them became sick. An examination of the situation led British officials to believe that it was arsenic poisoning causing the volatile illness. However, the culprit was probably incompetent, as he used too much of the poison in the bread dough. This resulted in the people who ate it to vomit out the poison. There were no casualties, but the intention was clear, and the British blamed Viceroy Ye's bounty for it. It didn't help that among the victims of this poisoning were Bowring and his wife and children. The poisoning caused hysteria and resulted in 500 arrests. The Chinese were charged with anything, even with looking suspicious. The false arrests scared the native population of Hong Kong, and more than half of them left the harbor city. The real culprit was never found, not even among the baker's employees who were directly involved in making the bread.

The *Arrow* incident, the *Thistle* massacre, and the arsenic poisoning were enough to give a reason for military action, something Bowring desired. He sent a letter to the governor-general of India to ask for reinforcements, as Seymour had only around 200 men besieging Canton. This was not enough, as Seymour didn't have enough people to invade the city; all he could do was bombard it from a distance. Back in London, Bowring's ambition for war found support, and the government ordered the governor-general of India to send a regiment and more artillery. Foreign Secretary George Villiers ordered Admiral Seymour to take Canton by all means. He was also to seize control of the Grand Canal and cut the rice supply to Peking. The plan was to starve the capital and force China into submission since all previous efforts of diplomacy fell on the emperor's deaf ears. The Crown now had new demands: a British embassy in Peking and more ports opened to British merchants and ships.

However, not everyone at home wanted another war with China. The United Kingdom lost an estimated ten million pounds in taxes and revenues in the First Opium War. The Tory opposition denounced the actions of Bowring and Parkes. They called them land-grabbers and usurpers of an independent and sovereign country. They also thought the *Arrow* incident wasn't a good enough reason for a new war. The leader of the Tory Party argued that since the *Arrow* had no British registration, it was officially a Chinese vessel and shouldn't have been protected by the British officials. He also accused Bowring and Parkes of intentionally provoking Chinese Viceroy Ye, who was nothing more than gentlemanlike, courteous, and respectful.

Although the Earl of Derby had many supporters in Parliament, no actions were taken to stop the escalation of the conflict. Lord Palmerston was again prime minister, and he was already known for his desire to increase British trade in the Chinese market and to legalize the importation of opium. He saw the Second Opium War as an opportunity to finally finish what he had started during the previous war. To ensure support for his cause, he started bribing various state officials. Even the loudest critics of the opium trade were silenced by Palmerston's bribes. But he didn't only use money to convince others to support him. He also promised high positions in government or elsewhere in return for silence or support. One such example is Lord

Shaftesbury, who was promised control over the election of new bishops. This appointment would bring a cathedral and vast amounts of land under his control.

Once the time for voting on the renewed war with China came, Prime Minister Palmerston gave his final speech. In it, he stated that when the Chinese boarded the *Arrow*, they took down the Union Jack to claim the ship as Chinese. It seems this angered Parliament members more than any other act of the incident, even more than the *Thistle* massacre. After all, the attack on the flag was regarded as an attack on Britain itself. Further on in his speech, Lord Palmerston spoke about the imbalance of trade with China and how selling them opium was the only way to pay off for the losses caused by the import of tea and silk. Then he turned to demonize Ye Mingchen, making him a public enemy of Britain. He talked about how the barbarian viceroy in Canton resorted to trickery, assassinations, and poison to humiliate the United Kingdom. He predicted that Ye would order a massacre of all Europeans in Canton if the British Parliament did nothing.

The voting public of Britain was inspired by the recent victory in the Crimean War, and the speech Lord Palmerston published was enough to push them into supporting the warmongering Whig Party. Although Palmerstone supported Bowring's efforts to incite the war in China, the governor of Hong Kong had formed an alliance with other members of Parliament, so someone else had to be appointed to lead the new negotiations with the emperor. For this position, James Bruce was chosen. He was the eighth Earl of Elgin and the twelfth Earl of Kincardine, previously serving as the governor of Jamaica and British North America.

A day before his departure to China, James Bruce received his orders from Foreign Minister Lord Clarendon. He was not to attack and claim Canton for the British, as Bowring and Seymour insisted. Instead, he needed to concentrate on acquiring the emperor's permission to set up a permanent British embassy in the imperial court in Peking. Their goal was to open up the path to direct negotiations with the court, instead of using the provincial governors as the emperor's liaisons. Besides the embassy, the British also ordered Lord Elgin to demand the opening of new ports to British traders and to push the Chinese to comply with the provisions of the Treaty of Nanjing. He was to use military aggression only as a last resort, and even then, he was to confine the fighting on the sea, where the British were superior.

Once Bruce landed in Singapore, where he was to take another ship to China, he was greeted with two letters, begging him to send the troops who were supposed to accompany him to India, where the Sepoy Mutiny (1857-1858) just broke out. Because these troops were reinforcements for the possible outbreak of a full-scale war in China, Lord Elgin didn't feel confident enough to continue his journey. Instead, he decided to wait in Singapore and experience firsthand the destructive effects opium had on people. He wandered the opium dens of Singapore, observing the addicts and coming to the conclusion that the drug was evil, as it made its consumers stupefied and useless.

On July 2nd, 1857, Lord Elgin arrived in Hong Kong, where Seymour pressed him to order an attack on Canton. As a backup, Seymour had a petition signed by eighty-five opium merchants who believed that if the British took Canton, the emperor would be forced to give them entry into new ports. The Earl of Elgin was under the impression that his compatriots were blinded by bloodlust and that only a total massacre in Canton would satisfy them. However, because his troops were still in India, Lord Elgin refused to listen to Seymour and the opium merchants.

Feeling insecure without the backup of his troops, Lord Elgin decided not to wait for their return but to personally go and get them from India. He sailed for Calcutta on July 14th, delaying his Chinese diplomatic business. There, he was shocked by the atrocities of war and the ability of his peers to torture and kill Indians, who falsely accused them of conspiring with rebels or of sexual abuse. While Lord Elgin was in India, Lord Bowring took it upon himself to write to Viceroy Ye. However, this was a strict violation of the orders he had received from London, which said that all communication between China and Britain had to be done through plenipotentiary Earl Lord Elgin. The relations of the two British officials thus became tensed.

One month after Lord Elgin's arrival, his French counterpart, Jean-Baptiste Louis Gros, also known as Baron Gros, landed in China. A year earlier, the French missionary Auguste Chapdelaine had been arrested for stirring up insurrection in China, and he was sentenced to death by beheading. However, he died in the small iron cage where he was kept before the execution. Nevertheless, he was still decapitated, and his head was hanged on a tree branch as a warning to other foreigners. France was furious about the murder of their missionary, and they used his death as an excuse to join Britain in the Second Opium War. Baron Gros and the Earl of Elgin both disliked Bowring, although they each had different opinions on how to proceed. While Gros wanted an immediate attack on Peking, Lord Elgin wanted to exhaust all diplomatic possibilities.

However, the foreign minister took Bowring's side, and in a letter to Lord Elgin, he ordered an attack on Canton. However, Gros was still against it, and he had to be convinced, as the British needed the help of French troops. Elgin left this task to Bowring, whose persistence proved fruitful. The French baron finally agreed.

In November of 1857, American Minister William Reed arrived in China on the steamship *Minnesota*, which was so huge that even though it had fifty guns, it was useless in the shallow rivers of China. However, it did manage to scare the Chinese forces with its immense size and power. America wanted to remain neutral in the Second Opium War, as both Reed and US President James Buchanan despised the opium trade. Reed's orders were not to get involved in the matters of the illegal drug trade or the war against Imperial China.

The Americans hoped to be mediators between the two warring sides and bring peace to China and Britain. So, when Viceroy Ye refused Reed an audition, the American diplomat decided to stay away from the conflict.

In December 1857, the French and British forces sailed into Canton Harbor. Lord Elgin and Gros each separately sent ultimatums to Ye. The French wanted the murderers of the missionary Auguste Chapdelaine brought to justice, reparations for the injustice, and permission to operate outside of the foreign quarter in Canton. Elgin decided not to mention the *Arrow* incident in his ultimatum. Instead, he demanded the emperor comply with the Treaty of Nanjing, which he had successfully ignored until now. The Earl of Elgin also didn't forget to demand a permanent embassy in Peking, as this was London's main interest. With a diplomat who would have direct access to court officials, in time, the British would manage to press the emperor to agree with their trade terms.

But both Gros and Elgin knew that Viceroy Ye had no power to accept or refuse their ultimatums. They also knew that any ultimatum sent to the emperor would only manage to anger him. Instead of answering, Ye decided to intimidate his opponents by beheading 400 Taiping rebels and displaying their heads on the city walls. Because he had no fleet or army to back him up, Ye hoped that the intimidation tactic would work and that the French and British would retreat. But his brutality backfired, as he only managed to provoke his enemies.

Chapter 8 – The Conflict Resumes

Viceroy Ye Mingchen arrested

(https://en.wikipedia.org/wiki/Second_Opium_War#/media/ File:1858,_Canton_Commissioner_Yeh_Men.jpg)

The two European officials, Gros and Elgin, supported by Russian Admiral Yevfimiy Putyatin, sent one last warning to Ye Mingchen, in which they said they would postpone the bombardment of Canton if he agreed to their demands. The Russians wanted direct access to the emperor, with whom they wanted to parley about ceding Manchuria. When the emperor declined to even admit them to his court, they decided to offer their help to the British. Ye had two days to answer the latest threat. While waiting, Gros and Lord Elgin turned the command over to Admiral Seymour and his French colleague, Admiral Charles Rigault de Genouilly. Gros retreated to safety, but the Earl of Elgin decided to wait for an answer at Canton Harbor, as he still hoped he could solve the China problem by diplomacy.

But the Chinese viceroy never bothered to reply, not even after the deadline was extended for three more days. On December 27th, 1857, with no reply coming, the attack on Canton began. A reconnaissance team was sent ashore under cover of night, and the next morning, the combined British and French fleet started shelling the city. The shooting did not stop for more than a day, and in all that time, the Chinese only responded with two shots. During the twenty-four hours of the bombardment, the loss of Chinese lives is estimated to have been 200, while the British and French forces didn't have any casualties. The might of the allied fleet was such that the whole city of Canton was burning.

Onshore, the 500 foot soldiers, both French and British, began their advance through the rice paddies as soon as the naval bombardment started. On their way toward the city, they had to go through a cemetery for criminals. Behind the tombstones, Chinese soldiers hid, and they opened fire on the passing allied troops. Unfortunately, they only had arrows, 16th-century matchlocks, and 18th-century muskets called gingalls, which were of no use against the superior armaments of the Europeans. To show their defiance, the Chinese waved yellow and red flags, the imperial colors. The Chinese soldiers were soon forced to retreat, and the allied Europeans took their position at the cemetery, using the tombstones as cover.

On the morning of December 29th, the soldiers were surprised to see that the Chinese army had retreated to the hill overlooking the city. It was a tactical mistake. On the hill, there was a magazine, which Ye was convinced the enemy would occupy first. However, once Ye emptied the city, the British and French were free to scale its walls with no one opposing them. Led by Admiral Rigault, the French were the first to scale the ladders and attack the city. There were some defenders on the Canton walls but not enough to put up any resistance. The Chinese tried to shell the allied forces from the top of the hill but to no avail. By 10 a.m., French and British flags were raised on top of the pagoda inside the city walls.

The naval bombardment of the city stopped for a moment to allow the land troops to invade the city. Once their men were in a safe position, Admiral Seymour ordered another shelling of the city from the sea. But after seeing the destroyed walls of Canton, the Earl of Elgin countermanded that order. He was convinced there was no need to continue, as he saw no tactical benefits for the bombardment. The French troops had thirty casualties by now, while the British had one hundred. However, the Chinese suffered the most. They had over 450 killed soldiers and an unknown number of wounded. Viceroy Ye was missing, and his second-in-command, Pih-kwei, distanced himself from the atrocities caused by his commander's disastrous policies.

On January 1st, 1858, Elgin decided to take a tour of Canton and assess the damage done to the city by himself. There was no resistance left in the city, and both British and French soldiers were looting everything they could find. Over 90 percent of Canton's population had fled the city, leaving all of their possessions behind for the taking. Lord Elgin tried to stop the looting, but he was powerless. The French wouldn't listen to him, and the British soldiers followed the lead of their brothers-in-arms. The Cohong merchants begged for the looting to stop, but nobody would listen to them. Despite Elgin's pleas to avoid the ransacking of homes, he ordered the looting of the city treasury, as it was considered legal plunder. After all, the war had to pay for itself. He confiscated fifty-two boxes of silver and sixty-eight boxes of gold ingots and taels, whose worth was equivalent to millions of dollars. The plunder was then sent to Calcutta as a war reparation prize.

On January 5th, Henry Parkes led a squad of one hundred Royal Marines to Ye's residency in the hopes of catching his nemesis. He even carried a small painting of the viceroy so he could recognize him, as he had never seen him personally. Ye had one of his subordinates imitate him and try to fool the British, but thanks to the painting, his trickery was seen through. Ye was caught while trying to climb the wall of his residency. He was arrested and sent to the steamship *Inflexible*, by which he would be sent to Calcutta. Once he arrived in India, Ye refused food and starved himself to death. However, his palace contained something even more valuable than the viceroy himself. The British found all of his correspondence with the imperial court in Peking, so they were now aware of all the emperor's thoughts and plans.

Pih-kwei was named governor of Canton by Gros and Elgin once he renounced Ye's actions. However, he was not to make any decisions without consulting the triumvirate, which was composed of Parkes, Captain Martineau, and Colonel Holloway. They had the power to veto all of Pih-kwei's edicts, and all the judiciary power was in their hands. The three were chosen because they were the only people of the entire combined British and French army who spoke Chinese. The language barrier had to be overcome if the Europeans were to control the city's hundreds of thousands of residents. Another attempt to secure cooperation between the Europeans and the Cantonese was the creation of a mixed police force, which was tasked with preventing the looting. This was especially welcomed by the merchants, who were eager to continue the trade within the city walls.

In March 1858, the Earl of Elgin left Canton and sailed for the mouth of the Bei He River with only two British and two French gunboats. Gros joined him there on April 20th, and four days later, Seymour brought two warships. Tan, the governor of Chihli province, received a joint message sent by the British, French, and Russian plenipotentiaries. It was an attempt to prevent the destruction of Canton through the use of a diplomatic approach. The message asked Tan to send a minister who would be able to negotiate with the European representatives. The governor of Chihli used the old Chinese tactic of stalling. In reality, he had no power to negotiate with the foreigners. However, he did pass the European demands on to the emperor, who immediately refused them all. Tan didn't mention this refusal to his enemies; instead, he chose to stall even more by promising to open new ports, as well as promising permission for foreign missionaries to spread Christianity.

While waiting at the mouth of the Bei He River, the Europeans received a visit from Archimandrite Palladius, a spiritual leader of the Russian Orthodox Church who had the emperor's permission to preach to a small community in Peking. On his way toward the European ships, Palladius made notes describing the position and strength of all the Chinese forces from Peking to their position. He also brought more good news: Peking was struck by famine, and the Xianfeng Emperor was ill due to opium use. He was also thinking of leaving the country so he could avoid dealing with the rebellion, war, and famine that struck his country. By late March, the combined Anglo-French fleet consisted of twenty-six gunboats, which were ready to attack the Dagu Forts (Taku Forts) that guarded the mouth of the river. The Europeans were less than one hundred miles from the Chinese capital. They could feel the approaching victory, but the Dagu Forts stood in their way.

The Dagu Forts were a set of five citadels defending the entrance into the Bei He River. Each was equipped with very antique artillery, and the Chinese defenders were aware of their weakness. To further fortify the citadels, they performed the stoic work of bringing thousands of sandbags from the river's shores. But this didn't help much. The Chinese were convinced the European alliance wouldn't dare enter the shallow river during low tide. But Admiral Seymour was willing to risk it, and he ordered a surprise attack on May 20th.

Previously, the Chinese set their cannons to shoot as if the tide was high, so when the alliance fleet started entering the river, the Dagu Fort defenders missed all of them. The two French warships, the *Mitraille* and *Fusee*, together with the British *Cormorant*, fired on the two forts on the left bank of the river. The British *Nimrod* and French *Avalance* and *Dragonne* shelled the three forts on the right bank. The Chinese lost around one hundred men, but they also managed to inflict some losses on their enemy. Five British soldiers and six French died from the gingalls, while sixty-two more were wounded.

Even before the alliance forces landed on the shores of the Bei He River, the Chinese defenders panicked and started deserting their posts. Desperate, the Manchu commander sent fifty fireboats at the foreigner's ships, but they crashed into the bank at the river bend, doing no damage to the enemy. The commander of the Dagu forces committed suicide at the Temple of the Sea God after failing to defend what was his. The angry emperor banished Tan, the governor of Chihli, into exile, condemning his failed efforts to defend the Dagu Forts.

In a military procession that resembled a triumph parade, Seymour and Rigault sailed their flotilla toward Tianjin, a city only thirty miles away from Peking. But the river was still shallow, and two of the biggest alliance ships had trouble passing through it. The *Cormorant* and the *Fusee* would often run aground. The Europeans were astonished to find the locals were more than pleased to pull the ships out of the shallows with their tugboats. They even refused any payment, but since a famine had hit the area, they were glad to accept some of the ship's rations. The locals were dissatisfied with their ruler's inability to deal with the famine, and they regarded the foreign fleet as a liberation force. Once the flotilla arrived at Tianjin, they met no resistance. The disheartened defenders heard the rumors that the emperor was overthrown, and they simply surrendered. The emperor wasn't overthrown, though; it was just a rumor. But after the loss of the Dagu Forts, the Xianfeng Emperor was ready to negotiate.

A retinue of court officials arrived in Tianjin to stop the alliance from reaching Peking. They were tasked with hosting the foreigners and starting the parley. A nearby temple, the Supreme Felicity, was turned into quarters for the foreigners, and the Europeans showed no respect for the Chinese culture. Instead of behaving like guests, they vandalized the temple, turning it into a bowling alley and washing in the sacred altars. Despite this, the emperor was serious in his will to achieve peace, and he sent his top courtiers and senior military officers: Guiliang (also known as Gui Liang) and the Mongol Hua Shan. On June 4th, 1858, Lord Elgin arrived at the meeting place accompanied by fifty marines as his bodyguards.

The negotiations between the Europeans and the Chinese lasted for over three weeks. The Chinese officials again employed their tactic of procrastination, as they feared angering their emperor. They had the power to accept all the terms, but they still wanted imperial approval so they could avoid the emperor's wrath. The clauses of the newly drawn treaty included the free passage of foreigners throughout China and permanent British and French embassies in Peking. These were immediately rejected by the Chinese officials, who stated that if they accepted, they would lose their lives. Baron Gros decided the French didn't need the embassy badly enough to continue fighting for it. He was ready to accept the peace terms if the Chinese officials agreed that the French diplomat would have access to Peking whenever he needed it.

Finally, Guiliang and Hua Shan accepted the terms of the Treaty of Tientsin (now known as the Treaty of Tianjin), opening up Tianjin, Nanjing, and nine more ports to the foreigners. The British also got four million silver taels (around 1,300,000 pounds) as war reparations, while the French got only half of that sum. The right to open an embassy in Peking was given to Britain, France, Russia, and neutral

America, although this would prove to be the problematic point of the treaty.

Even though Lord Elgin was ordered by the prime minister of Britain to acquire permission to sell opium in China, the Earl of Elgin refused to even bring up this question during the negotiations. The Americans did recommend the legalization of the drug because they saw it as a new trade item that could be taxed. They also argued that if China's tax on opium was high enough, it would make it a drug of the elite, reducing the number of people addicted to it.

The Chinese agreed to the proposal of American Minister Reed, and they planned to implement a tax of sixty taels per chest. But the British needed that tax lower because their business thrived due to the number of addicts. They wanted to drop the tax to thirty taels per chest, which would make it lower than the already existing tax on tea and silk. The merchant companies fully supported the British stand on the matter, and they lobbied hard in Parliament so they could get the tax of thirty taels. The French showed expertise in knowing the facts about opium, but they didn't care about its trade. What they wanted from China was the legalization of the coolie trade. Their treaty with China had a clause that, in effect, legalized the kidnapping and indentured servitude forced upon the Chinese.

Russia was the first to agree with China. They were satisfied with not having a permanent embassy in Peking because their largest interest, the swap of territories in Siberia, was approved by the emperor. However, Britain and France couldn't agree to visitation rights for their ambassadors, and they felt as if Russia had betrayed them. Five days later, the Americans, who stayed neutral during the conflict, signed an agreement as well. Theirs was the same as Russia's but with the clause of religious freedom defined more accurately. The American missionaries were free to preach Christianity anywhere in China. Both Russia and America included the most-favored-nation clause, which gave them the right to adjust the treaty at a later point, depending on what concessions the other countries received.

The French treaty with China was almost identical to the American and Russian ones, but Baron Gros hesitated to sign it, as he didn't want to undercut Elgin's negotiations. The British had two clauses of the treaty they desperately wanted to include: a permanent embassy in Peking and freedom for their citizens to travel anywhere in China. Because they could not reach an agreement upon these clauses, the negotiations prolonged for two weeks after Russia and America had already signed theirs. The Chinese commissioners couldn't accept these clauses because they had strict orders from the emperor not to do so; if they did, they would face execution. Finally, after six weeks of parleying, the British treaty was ratified on June 26th, 1858. A large portion of China was opened for British trade, and the Christian missionaries could preach anywhere in the country. In Shanghai, a follow-up meeting was held to set up the taxes on imported goods. The two countries reached an agreement and set the tax at 5 percent. Among the taxed items, besides silk, ceramics, and tea, was opium itself. However, when the Treaty of Tianjin was brought before the Xianfeng Emperor, he refused to sign it, as it was simply too humiliating for China.

Chapter 9 – The Advance

The ruins of a Dagu Fort
(https://en.wikipedia.org/wiki/Felice_Beato#/media/File:Felice_Beato
_(British,_born_Italy)_-_(Interior_of_the_Angle_of_Taku
_North_Fort_Immediately_After_Its_Capture_by_Storm)_-
_Google_Art_Project.jpg)

While the British, French, Americans, and Russians celebrated their treaties, the humiliated Xianfeng Emperor sent a missive to the viceroy of Canton, Huang Zonghan, with the task to incite a rebellion. In July 1858, the inhabitants of the city took up arms. They managed to secure the artillery and shelled the British residents settled in Whampoa. By July 21", they even raided Canton. Upon receiving the news in Shanghai, Lord Elgin and the other British officials who were reviewing the Treaty of Tianjin demanded the Chinese commissioners bring Huang to justice.

To demonstrate Britain's new right to travel anywhere in China, the Earl of Elgin decided to tour the Yangtze River for the next two months. He boarded a survey boat and was followed by two gunboats that served as protection. The fact that the Taiping rebels, who had settled in Nanjing, fired on his retinue during the tour proved his wisdom in bringing the defensive gunboats. Angered that the Treaty of Tianjin was being ignored so soon after its signing in Shanghai, Elgin ordered his men to bombard the rebel city for ninety minutes. Lord Elgin planned to enter Peking at the end of his tour and present Queen Victoria's letter to the emperor himself, but the development of hostilities in Canton made him turn back.

In February 1859, Chinese guerilla forces ambushed and massacred 700 British marines stationed in the countryside near Canton. In response, the British troops stationed in Canton, which numbered around 3,000, marched on the guerilla camp at Shektsing and razed it to the ground. Soon, the emperor ordered the removal of Huang and the dispersal of the guerilla forces.

Lord Elgin left China in March 1859, meeting in Sri Lanka with his brother, Frederick Bruce, who had just been appointed the first ambassador of China. The title should have belonged to Lord Elgin himself, as his efforts brought about the Treaty of Tianjin and the de facto legalization of opium. However, he was tired of the Far East, and he declined the offer when it was proposed to him at an earlier date. Frederick Bruce wasn't without his credentials, and he wasn't assigned to the ambassadorial post just because he was Lord Elgin's brother. He had been the governor of Newfoundland, and since 1844, he was the colonial secretary in Hong Kong. This position in Hong Kong gave him much-needed experience with Chinese culture, customs, and eccentricities.

He arrived at the mouth of the Bei He River on June 18th, 1859, with sixteen warships, which were tasked with making the Chinese emperor comply with the Treaty of Tianjin. Bruce was also accompanied by the American ambassador John E. Ward, who came with only one steamer, the *Powhatan*. French representative Anton de Bourbelon showed up with two ships, but his whole fleet was stationed in nearby Indo-Chinese waters.

The Xianfeng Emperor was stubborn in not allowing the foreigners to enter Peking, and he suggested ratifying the Treaty of Tianjin in Shanghai, but all three representatives declined this offer. To block the foreign powers from entering the capital, construction of three thick bamboo walls began. Bruce hoped to avoid another conflict, and he wrote to Peking, asking the imperial officials to remove the blockade. When the reply never came, he ordered the destruction of the walls. The first one was easy to go through, but the second and third proved more resistant. While the British forces were stuck, the Chinese repaired the first one under cover of night. The following day, when Bruce ordered another attack on the walls, the Chinese stationed on the river shore attacked with their forty stationary guns. This time, they had better luck in aiming, and nine British marines lost their lives.

The Chinese defenses were able to disable five of the enemy's gunships. The neutral Americans joined the battle once they heard the British were in trouble. Commodore Josiah Tattnall of the American fleet rushed to the rescue, with his ship, the *Toeywhan*, hauling another ship that carried 200 American soldiers. The British and French commanders landed their troops in front of one of the Dagu Forts, which were returned to the Chinese during the Tianjin negotiations. But the European troops were stuck in the mud, and the Chinese had no trouble shooting them with their primitive, short-range gingalls. The British and French forces had to retreat to the safety of their ships.

For the first time during the Opium Wars, the allied forces suffered unusually high numbers of casualties: 500 dead and at least as many wounded. One of the gunboats, the *Kestrel*, was destroyed, and it sank to the bottom of the river, while another three were disabled. Bruce realized that pushing the attack on the Dagu Forts, without the proper reinforcements, would be fatal for his troops. The British, French, and Americans were utterly surprised by this sudden Chinese competence. To save face, Bruce wrote to London, blaming the Russians for allying with the Chinese. He even claimed that eyewitnesses saw Russian fur hats commanding the Chinese troops on the walls of the forts. To excuse their first defeat during the Opium Wars, Lord Palmerston accepted Bruce's explanation. But the truth was that there were no Russians involved in the Chinese defenses. The defense was commanded by Prince Senggelinqin alone, a Mongol nobleman who warned the emperor not to be overly optimistic because this was just one victory in a series of defeats.

Back in Britain, the news of the defeat at the Dagu Forts brought out the bloodthirsty public. The newspapers were calling for revenge, and they exaggerated the number of British casualties. Lord Palmerston supported Bruce's idea that the Russians were involved with the defense of the forts, but he was unable to decide what their next move should be. Attacking Peking was an option, but the task was of immense magnitude, and it would demand a huge number of British forces. The casualties were sure to be even greater. Another option was cutting off the Grand Canal's food supply to Peking or the occupation of Chusan province. The latter would have to be done together with the French, and this was an alliance Palmerston wanted to avoid. But the press continued to call for reprisal. The London *Times* wrote that since China was not respecting the Treaty of Tianjin, the British, with or without the French, had to teach the pagans a lesson. Similarly, the *Daily Telegraph* demanded revenge for the fallen British soldiers.

The only one who remained faithful to his conviction that the war was bad for Britain was the Chancellor of the Exchequer, William Ewart Gladstone. He argued that the war was too costly and that the British economy would suffer if the conflict continued. At the Cabinet meeting on September 17th, 1859, Gladstone opposed the press's call for revenge, stating that Bruce's task should be to press China to respect the Treaty of Tianjin, not to pursue a war. Lord Elgin was present at the meeting, as he was now occupying the position of postmaster general. He disagreed with his brother's intention to invade Peking, but he chose to keep silent during the meeting. However, he was convinced he had the solution to the China problem, and he had to voice it. Lord Elgin wrote a memo to the Cabinet, where he proposed to block the Bei He River instead of the Grand Canal. This would have the same effect, as the rice would be unable to reach the capital. The Bei He River was a better position, as the British forces wouldn't have to risk and engage in combat along the Yangtze. Lord Elgin hoped to starve the Manchu dynasty into submission but not to topple it so that the God-worshipping Taiping rebels could take over.

But Elgin was wrong about one thing. The Bei He River was only used for the transportation of rice. The capital would still be able to feed its people with corn or beans, which were plentiful in the northern parts of China. Rice was a staple only in the south, and it is very unlikely the emperor would have missed a side dish on his plate. None of the members of the Cabinet knew China well enough, though, so they agreed to Lord Elgin's proposal. The message was sent to Bruce to demand an apology for the British losses at the Dagu Forts, reparations for the war in an unspecified amount, and respect for the Treaty of Tianjin. He was to give thirty days for the Chinese officials to accept the terms, and if they refused, he was to go with his brother's plan and block the Bei He River. The letter reached Bruce in January 1860, but Elgin's plan had another problem. The blockade of the river would be useless at this point since the ships wouldn't sail for Peking until spring. Bruce was smart enough to delay the demand until March, but the Chinese emperor rejected it anyway.

It seems that the British public, which had so vehemently called for bloodthirsty retribution against the Chinese, grew tired by the spring of 1860. The casualties of the Dagu Forts were already old news, and there was no interest in the diplomatic efforts between Britain and China. Even the debates in Parliament regarding the China issue were held in a desultory fashion. The merchants whose business depended on opium wanted the conflict with China to be over, as it only managed to alienate their business partners, the Cohong merchants.

The failure of Frederick Bruce to achieve anything in China did not result in his replacement. However, he was demoted, as the new top British emissary to China was on his way. It was none other than his brother, the Earl of Elgin. In April 1860, Lord Elgin was ordered to take the lead in the negotiations with China. If he saw fit, he had permission to continue with the war. His orders were to demand the reparations for the war, the apology for the loss at the Dagu Forts, and the compliance of Peking with the Treaty of Tianjin. However, Britain was willing not to pursue the issue of a permanent embassy within the imperial court. Lord Elgin was only to reintroduce this matter if the negotiations went well.

Baron Gros was also called back to serve in China, and Elgin was happy to meet his old friend again. The British sent an impressive number of troops with him. Combined with the French, it was a military force to be reckoned with. However, the relations between the two nations were not at their best. In France, Napoleon III, the nephew of Napoleon I Bonaparte, was in power. His expansion of the empire sparked many rumors in Britain, and one of them was that he planned to invade the Kowloon Peninsula just north of Hong Kong. To prevent this, Harry Parkes was ordered to negotiate a permanent lease of this area with the Chinese viceroy. The annual fee for the lease of Kowloon was set at 500 silver taels (160 pounds). The peaceful conclusion of the Kowloon agreement was reached on March 18th, 1860, and it was a paradoxical event, considering that at the time, the British were planning an invasion of Peking.

The Chinese were optimistic that the Dagu Forts would again stop the British advance on Peking. Their enthusiasm wasn't lessened when they learned the British had a Chinese brigade among their army. These were coolies from Hong Kong who volunteered to fight on the side of the foreigners. For their betrayal, they were paid a high amount of nine dollars per month, and they proved to be worthy of the investment. They were a versatile brigade, eager to fight against their own countrymen. Coolies usually came from the bottom of Chinese society, so serving the foreigners was their way of repaying Imperial China back for all the mistreatment they had to endure. However, the British didn't feel comfortable serving next to the Chinese, and they were afraid to arm them with rifles. Instead, they gave them bamboo staves as weapons. The Chinese defenders armed with antique matchlocks looked far superior when compared to the coolie attackers. Still, the British officers found the coolies to be one of the best brigades in the Second Opium War.

The first target of the renewed Anglo-French army was the island of Chusan. An army of 2,000 British and 500 French was sent to take the island, which would give them control over the Yangtze River. Fortunately for the Europeans, they encountered no resistance. The people of Chusan surrendered without a fight. The same happened fifty miles to the north. Shanghai welcomed the allies without a fight, the reason being that its defenders were away fighting the Taiping rebels at Fuzhou. The Chinese officials in Shanghai hoped the Europeans would aid them against the rebels, even though they planned to invade China. This was a clear sign that the provincial leaders were left on their own to fight the rebels, as the emperor was unable to quell the rebellion that raged all over the country. The allied forces promised they would defend Shanghai if the Taiping rebels decided to invade it, but they would not send their troops against the rebels unnecessarily. To show their goodwill, the British marines patrolled the waters around the city, while the French guarded its gates. The antique Chinese artillery on the city walls were replaced with modern British cannons.

The Bruce brothers reunited in Shanghai, where the planning for the future course of the war began. In July, 150 British ships, under the command of General Sir James Hope Grant, landed at Beitang, near the Dagu Forts. They were soon joined by the French, under the command of General Charles Cousin-Montauban. It took them five days to unload all the troops and equipment from the more than 200 ships. The Beitang Fort was empty, and there was no one to fire on the invaders. Once they entered the fort's walls, the Europeans found out why it was deserted. The guns stationed as a defensive measure were wooden replicas designed to scare the attackers. The city itself housed around 20,000 people, who welcomed the allies as liberators, and they were even willing to show where the Chinese defenders had buried mines. However, their welcome was repaid with the looting of their houses and the raping of their women. With nowhere to go, the women of Beitang chose to poison themselves or even drown instead of enduring the sexual assaults from the British and French soldiers.

The first to take the blame was the coolies who served in the allied army. General Grant accused them of being opium addicts who couldn't control themselves. But the atrocities committed in Beitang were the fault of all nations. The Sikh, British, and French soldiers proved no better than their Chinese volunteers. To restore the discipline, the British officers ordered the flogging of thirty soldiers. The rest complied to escape a similar fate.

On August 3rd, 1860, the allied forces moved toward Tianjin, where the cavalry of Prince Senggelinqin blocked their way. Even though the Chinese were armed with only arrows, spears, and 18th-century flintlocks, the allies had no cavalry to match them, and they had to retreat. The Mongol prince sent letters to Peking, proclaiming a great victory against the European invaders, but the British weren't idle. General Grant set about assembling a cavalry, and he managed to do so in less than ten days. Eight hundred soldiers were given horses and ordered to attack the Chinese from behind, while the main force of the allied army would lead the attack head-on. The British had three new Armstrong guns, whose explosions were enough to scatter the Chinese cavalry. However, Prince Senggelinqin had a strong grip on his men. The remaining cavalry continued to approach the invader's main army, confronting the guns that continued to blast them. Finally, they were halted at around 450 yards, and the Europeans had to admire the suicidal bravery of the Chinese. It was the Sikhs' guns that finally made the Chinese cavalry run back to the safety of the Dagu Forts. The Sikh cavalry wanted to pursue the fleeing enemy, but the mud prevented their horses from running, and the tired soldiers had to give up.

Approaching the Dagu Forts, British General Hope Grant and French General Cousin-Montauban disagreed on how they should proceed. While Cousin-Montauban wanted to attack all four forts at once, the British military leader had a plant to single them out and take them down one by one. The disagreement was settled when the opportunity to take the Danggu village arose. This village was in a perfect position, as it would allow them to single out and neutralize the northern fort first. Lord Elgin accompanied the allied forces, and he was eager to observe the upcoming attack from atop the temple, which was stationed in the middle of the village. However, Grant saved his life by noticing that the temple was within firing range from the fort's walls.

The attack began on August 21st after both British and French guns started bombarding the northern Dagu Fort. They were providing cover for the men and horses dragging the Armstrong guns and other artillery to within 600 feet from the fort's wall, where they would be most effective. The Chinese defenders were quickly neutralized, having nothing else but gingalls and matchlocks to fight the invaders. At around 6 a.m., a lucky British bullet managed to hit a gunpowder store within the fort. The massive explosion was a decisive moment in the battle, as for the next half an hour, the Chinese couldn't return fire. This time window was enough for the French troops to scale the walls. With a bayonet charge at the top of the fort's walls, the French easily dispatched the rest of the defenders. The British guns managed to blow a hole in the wall, and the soldiers poured in, finishing off the fleeing Chinese. Even though it seemed as if the victory came easy, the casualties within the British and French ranks were unusually high, reaching over 400 dead or wounded. But the Chinese lost almost 2,000 men in the Third Battle of Dagu Forts (also known as Taku Forts). Over 9,000 survivors remained in the fort, and they surrendered to French General Collineau. Not knowing what to do with so many prisoners of war, he decided to free them.

The psychological effect of the fort's fall on the Chinese military leaders proved to be beneficial to the allies. Instead of continuing the fight, the Chinese commanders proposed to open the way for the foreigner's fleet to enter Tianjin, where they could meet the emperor's envoys and continue negotiations. However, the British couldn't agree to another useless parley at Tianjin. Instead, they were determined to reach Peking. After a series of threats, the remaining three Dagu Forts surrendered without a single drop of blood. The way to Tianjin was opened, and on August 23rd, the invaders entered the city, which surrendered immediately, as there were no defenders left.

In Tianjin, Lord Elgin and Baron Gros discussed their strategy. Inspired by their previous victory and the surrender of the city, they came up with a new set of demands for the emperor. They wanted a formal apology for the defeat of the British and French forces at the Dagu Forts back in 1859. They also demanded double the amount of reparation money and the confirmation of the Treaty of Tianjin. They also wanted permanent control of Tianjin, which would allow the allied forces to create an artificial famine whenever they needed to keep the Chinese emperor in control. However, neither Elgin nor Gros mentioned a permanent embassy in Peking. They feared that this would be the demand that would anger the Xianfeng Emperor and prompt him to decline all the other demands.

These terms caused a panic in Peking, and once again, Guiliang was sent to lead the negotiations. However, he was so intimidated by the demands that he resorted to procrastination. This time, the Chinese tactic was to Elgin's and Gros's benefit, as it bought them time to gather their forces outside of Tianjin and prepare for the march on Peking.

Chapter 10 – Burning the Palace and Diplomacy

One of the Summer Palace complex buildings
before being burned down

(https://en.wikipedia.org/wiki/Felice_Beato#/media/File:Belvedere_of
_the_God_of_Literature,_Summer_Palace,_Beijing,_6%E2%80%931
8_October,_1860.jpg)

It didn't take long for Lord Elgin to persuade Baron Gros to join him and the troops on their march to the capital city of China. Gros wanted to stay in the safety of Tianjin, but once he saw the fear in the Chinese diplomat's eyes, he decided to be present when Peking was taken. On their way to the capital, the European leaders received numerous letters from the imperial court. In them, various court officials begged them to stop their advance and explained how Guiliang was confused. The emperor would accept all the terms if they refrained from entering the sacred city. But Elgin refused to stop, and he said he would meet the royal officials in Peking's suburbs of Tongxian. The Chinese begged him to meet them halfway between Tianjin and Peking, at the town of Hesewu. Gros liked this idea, but Elgin firmly refused.

In the end, the allied army had to stop at Hesewu because it was almost impossible to supply the men with food. Lord Elgin was pushing his soldiers forward at such a pace that the ration wagons couldn't keep up. But Elgin couldn't allow a delay. Instead, he sent Parkes to Tongxian to meet Cai and Muyin, the Manchu officials. Cai was the emperor's cousin, and Muyin was the president of the Board of War. Their high ranks served to prove that the emperor took the situation seriously and was ready to negotiate without further delays. The parley lasted for eight hours, but Parkes managed to persuade both officials to accept all of the European terms.

In Peking, the Xianfeng Emperor couldn't make up his mind whether he should fight or flee. Even the commander of the Imperial Army, Prince Senggelinqin, advised him that it wasn't a time for valor and that the emperor should think about his safety first. He urged the Xianfeng Emperor to leave the capital and go north, where the imperial hunting grounds were. There, the ruler could enjoy the pastime sport while waiting for his representatives to take care of the invasion. Some historians speculate that Senggelinqin wanted to usurp the throne in the emperor's absence, but the majority agree that the general didn't want the emperor to be taken as a hostage, as that would put them in an impossible situation. The only person at the royal court displaying bravery was Imperial Consort Cixi. She advised the Xianfeng Emperor to remain in Peking and lead his people. Encouraged by his favorite consort's bravery, the Xianfeng Emperor proposed to ride in front of a huge army and intimidate the Europeans. After this display of courage, he would depart to his hunting grounds at Rehe.

In Tongxian, Cai and Muyin approved the allied force's encampment. They even allowed Elgin and Gros to enter Peking with a retinue of 2,000 soldiers. However, the Chinese officials refused to deliver Queen Victoria's letter to the Xianfeng Emperor. However, on his way back to confer with Elgin and Gros, Parkes noticed that the Manchu cavalry was gathering where the allied army was supposed to camp in Tongxian. He sent a messenger back to Tianjin with the news of the gathering Chinese army, while he turned back to confront Cai and Muyin. However, in their place, Parkes was awaited by Prince Senggelinqin, who immediately had him arrested.

General Grant feared that an attack on the Chinese would cost Parkes his life. However, he was pressed by the French, who didn't care about a British diplomat, and so, an attack was launched on September 18th, 1860. The allied army numbered around 3,500 men, who faced about 20,000 Manchu troops.

One last attempt at diplomacy was made before the battle began. Accompanied by a mounted escort, Thomas Wade, a diplomat and interpreter, was sent to ask the Mongol prince to release Parkes. However, Parkes was already suffering over a century-old issue between the British and the Chinese. After he refused to kowtow to Prince Senggelinqin, the ruthless Manchu smashed his head against the marble floor multiple times. In his defiance, Parkes was the last European to bow to Chinese officials during the Opium Wars, even though it was involuntary. After he refused to write to his superiors, Elgin and Gros, Parkes was thrown into prison.

After a week of torture, Parkes was transferred to an individual cell with much better living conditions. He was treated better, and the daily tortures stopped. He wasn't even asked to bow to the officials when they came to interrogate him. Soon, he realized this was because they needed him. It was a sign the war wasn't going well for the Chinese, and they wanted him to intervene and write to Lord Elgin to stop the attack on Peking. He agreed but only under the condition that he and his comrades were released from prison. In his letters to Elgin, Parkes refused to make any pleas. On October 6th, he and the other prisoners of war were released a few days before the order for their execution by the Xianfeng Emperor arrived.

The allied forces gathered outside of Tongxian. Prince Senggelinqin's cavalry numbered 20,000, but as before, this wasn't a battle in which numbers matter: it was a battle where state-of-the-art weaponry and tactics reigned supreme. The Chinese mostly used bows and arrows, and they had only a handful of ancient muskets. Besides their weapons, their tactics were also medieval. Prince Senggelinqin relied on trapping the enemy and going in for the kill. However, he would need to stretch his army to encircle the Europeans, which would expose his men and allow the enemy to easily penetrate the trap.

As the Manchu soldiers spread out, preparing to encircle their enemy, the allies took the opportunity and attacked their weakest point. The Sikh cavalry, led by General Cousin-Montauban, attacked the left flank of the Chinese troops, while the French infantry assaulted the Chinese camp. Almost effortlessly, the Sikhs penetrated the Chinese ranks and caused panic. The use of the Armstrong guns by the French infantry caused a commotion in which the Mongol cavalry dispersed. The Sikhs chased the retreating Chinese, massacring them with bayonets. Almost 1,500 Manchu died that day, while the allies only lost 35 men.

Tongxian fell on September 21st after a short bayonet battle. The French troops secured the Baliqiao bridge, which crossed the canal that divided this town from Peking. Now under a real threat of invasion, the Chinese warned they would execute the prisoners if the attack continued. But Cousin-Montauban pressed the attack, ignoring the threats. The Chinese defenders jumped into the canal, fearing for their lives. Again, the casualties showed the superiority of the European troops. While the Chinese lost 2,000 men, the French troops only had three casualties.

General Grant had a slightly more difficult victory than his French counterpart. Unfortunately, he mistook the Mongol cavalry in the distance for French troops, and he didn't order the attack. The Mongols thought the British were cowards, and they charged. Once the British realized it was the enemy approaching them, they started shooting with the deadly Armstrong guns, dispersing the Mongol cavalry. Luck was with the British, as they suffered no casualties.

After the fall of Tongxian, Prince Senggelinqin panicked and fled the capital, taking the remnants of the Imperial Army with him. He made camp outside of the northwestern city wall, but he posed no real threat to the allies. By taking the two bridges that led to Peking, the way to the capital was completely open for the Europeans. Peking's only defense was the soldiers with antique guns on the top of the thick walls. Grant feared that the allies' artillery wouldn't be enough to breach the city walls, especially if the citizens of Peking joined the fight. The attack was halted until heavy siege guns arrived from Tianjin.

In the meantime, Lord Elgin wanted to try negotiating once more. This time, he got to deal with someone from the top of the imperial administration: Prince Gong. He was the Xianfeng Emperor's younger brother, and he proved to be more capable. When Lord Elgin asked him to release the prisoners of war to move the negotiations forward, Prince Gong answered he would release them only after the allies withdrew from Peking. He also said the prisoners would be executed in the public square the moment Peking was assaulted.

The siege guns needed to blast the walls of the capital arrived on October 5th. The Xianfeng Emperor had already left the city, along with a majority of the royal army. Prince Gong was left to defend Peking with only a fraction of the Imperial Army. The first shots echoed in the early morning of October 7th, 1860. A day earlier, French and British troops marched around the city from opposite sides, meeting at the Summer Palace, which lay just outside of the walls. The French reached the meeting place first and were surprised to learn it was abandoned. No one was waiting to defend the emperor's property, except for 500 eunuchs who bravely launched an attack. But they were not soldiers, and they had no weapons. After the French soldiers killed twenty of them, the rest fled.

Calling it a Summer Palace is an understatement, as it was a complex of 200 buildings and included a vast park dotted with various tents, pavilions, and lakes. The complex hid many treasures, and it was fortunate the French arrived first, as they were more interested in looting than vandalizing like the British soldiers. The Summer Palace served as a storehouse for the tributes received by the Chinese emperors for centuries. The complex also housed a vast library that was about to be lost forever. The French realized what a treasure was in their possession, and they very carefully began picking it apart and storing it for transport. But greed prevailed, and soon, they abandoned the preservation of the items and buildings and turned to ripping and demolishing the palace walls to grab as much as they could before the British arrived. The looting was of such intensity that Cousin-Montauban later found himself questioned by a special French committee that investigated the damage caused by the looting. Even the famous writer Victor Hugo condemned the French commander for not stopping his soldiers from looting and destroying the Summer Palace.

The British arrived at the Summer Palace on the afternoon of October 7th, 1860. Grant later testified that by the time his troops arrived, the palace was already stripped of its most precious items. He mocked Cousin-Montauban's inability to control his soldiers, but in reality, Grant couldn't prevent the British troops from looting and vandalizing the palace either. It was the British officers who started destroying the palace, shooting at priceless antique mirrors. When Lord Elgin finally arrived, he was shocked by the destruction. Many artifacts, whose value will never be known, were lost to the aggressiveness of both the French and British soldiers.

When Harry Parkes was released on October 8th, Lord Elgin felt relieved. It seems that he didn't care about the fates of the other forty prisoners of war still in Chinese hands, as he ordered a full-scale attack on Peking the next morning. Trenches were dug in front of the An Tung Gate, where the artillery was brought. The allies threatened to bombard the city if the gate was not opened. Elgin gave the Chinese time to consult with the faraway emperor, with the deadline set for October 24th. When the deadline was reached, Elgin prepared to bombard the city, but the gate opened wide, letting the invaders in without a single shot fired. At the head of 500 men, Elgin entered Peking as a conqueror.

While waiting for the emperor's response, the Chinese released one French and two Sikh soldiers. They were in such bad shape that the Sikh soldier died the next day. Over the next few days, the Chinese would release more prisoners in small numbers. Most of them were already dead, so the coffins containing their bodies were delivered to the allies. These men had been forced to kneel, with their hands bound, for days without food or water while exposed to the elements. Gangrene and infections took the lives of many British and French prisoners, who perished in excruciating pain. Angered, Elgin and Gros demanded retribution for their lost comrades. While the French baron was satisfied with monetary compensation, the British earl needed an act of bloodthirsty revenge. However, he agreed that no more blood should be spilled, and he satisfied himself with ordering the Summer Palace to be burned to the ground, which took place on October 18th, 1860. This was a punishment that damaged the honor of the Chinese emperor but one that preserved lives.

While Elgin's actions were celebrated by the British public, as he was now the war hero who humiliated the foreign emperor without spilling blood, Queen Victoria condemned the burning of the Summer Palace. Burning a royal residence hit close to home, and she believed Elgin shouldn't be praised for this cultural vandalism. However, for the next century, the Earl of Elgin would be celebrated for the victory over the Chinese in the Second Opium War. The Summer Palace was restored by Empress Dowager Cixi between 1884 and 1895 in celebration of her sixtieth birthday. The Summer Palace, a landscape monument that combines natural beauty with artificial design, became a UNESCO world heritage site in 1998 and is open to the public today.

Once he was triumphantly inside the capital, General Grant advised Elgin not to linger in Peking, as winter was approaching. Grant was against wintering in the city because the Chinese guerilla forces could easily starve the capital by cutting its connection with food supplies all over the country. The peace agreement needed to be reached quickly so that the allied army could retreat to the safety of Tianjin. Cousin-Montauban agreed with his British friend, and he also reminded Elgin that Prince Senggelinqin was still stationed outside the city walls, threatening the success of the parley. But the Xianfeng Emperor cut off all correspondence with his Manchu administrators in Peking, and the task of saving Peking fell on Prince Gong alone.

On October 24th, Lord Elgin met with Prince Gong to sign the Convention of Peking. After learning from the Chinese that he was a target of assassination, Elgin showed up at the meeting with 500 soldiers, who were not just there as his bodyguards but also served the purpose of showing off his power. He didn't forget to insult the prince, who had lost the city without a fight. Elgin also came with eight porters, a number reserved, by Chinese tradition, only for the emperor. Prince Gong, according to his ranks, was followed by only six porters. Although they were humiliated, the Chinese officials couldn't object. Prince Gong signed the treaty, and an Italian photographer was brought along to preserve the scene for history. The portrait shots of Earl Elgin and Prince Gong captured by Signor Felice Beato, one of the first war photographers in the world, sadly didn't survive the destruction of time.

The Europeans simply gave Prince Gong the documents to sign, as they decided would not listen to negotiations. The British document included the emperor's official apology for the aggression with ten million dollars as reparations to Britain. The British ambassador would be allowed permanent residency in Peking. In addition, the territory across Hong Kong, which was known as Kowloon, was ceded to the British. Tianjin was added to the list of ports that would be opened to foreign merchant ships, and the freedom of religion was established in China, allowing foreign missionaries to preach Christianity across the country. British ships were allowed to enter the coolie trade and carry the captive Chinese to the shores of America. And finally, the cause of the war—opium—was legalized in China. Although he was humiliated, Prince Gong signed the document and invited the British conquerors to a banquet, but Lord Elgin declined out of fear of being poisoned.

The signing of the French version of the convention occurred the day after, and Baron Gros refrained from insulting his imperial host. Instead, he gifted Prince Gong with a collection of French coins and signed photos of Napoleon III and his wife, Empress Eugénie. Even though the French had nothing to do with the burning of the Summer Palace, Baron Gros was gracious enough to apologize for the event. Unlike Elgin, Gros accepted Prince Gong's offer of a banquet, and no one was poisoned.

The Earl of Elgin remained in Shanghai until January 1861, after which he returned to Britain, never to step foot on Chinese soil again. He was a hero back in England and was rewarded with a promotion to the viceroy of India the next year. However, he only remained in that position for less than two years, as he died of an aneurysm in November 1864. The Xianfeng Emperor died only a year after signing the Convention of Peking. He was humiliated to the point where he decided never to return to the capital city. Instead, he remained in Rehe, where he indulged in the destructive opium until his death. Queen Victoria received a present that originated from the ruins of the Summer Palace. A captain found a little dog wandering the ruins, and upon returning to London, he decided to give it to the queen. The dog was Pekingese, and she named it Looty, a rather distasteful name.

After the Second Opium War, Empress Cixi organized a modernization effort, known as the Self-Strengthening Movement. However, she remained one of the most stubborn and traditional leaders of China. This country was ravaged by another revolution, and it seems that after the Western powers subdued the imperial court, the Qing dynasty could not recuperate. The empire's weakness was evident, and it would only take fifty-two years until the last emperor of China, Puyi, abdicated and left the country in the grasp of the Chinese Communist Party.

As for the drug itself, it soon became the equivalent of money. Merchants found it useful, as they could buy other products using opium instead of silver. Opium's worth soon fell so much that its value was estimated in copper. Poppies, from which this drug is derived, can be grown everywhere. It thrives in any soil and all weather conditions. Chinese farmers started replacing their unpredictable rice and corn crops with poppy, even though the Qing dynasty continued its opium suppression efforts. The viceroys of provinces often ignored imperial edicts that banned the cultivation of poppy so they could get rich from bribes. They were also reluctant to anger the farmers, whose only source of income after a particularly bad rice harvest would be their poppy crops.

Britain opposed the production of opium inside China since that meant the demand for Indian opium would drop. British pressure resulted in the Qing dynasty sending special commissioners to the provinces that grew poppy to oversee the destruction of the fields. However, even these commissioners soon became dependent on opium bribes, and they would often turn a blind eye to its production. The last effort of the Qing dynasty to suppress opium came in 1901, but by then, even the British had given up on the drug trade. They were pushed out of the market by the domestic growers and merchants. Britain signed a treaty in 1907 in which it agreed to stop importing opium to China, while the emperor promised to eradicate domestic production. However, once the Chinese government fell in 1911, the farmers and merchants returned to their lucrative opium business. By 1933, people of all social levels were addicted to opium again, and by 1940, the government was actively selling the drug to Japanese-inhabited provinces.

It was Mao's government (1943–1976) that suppressed opium successfully. During the 1950s, the ruthless Communist Party of China executed any opium dealers they caught and destroyed all the opium-producing fields, which were then replanted with food crops. Around 10,000 addicts were forced to abandon their opium habits, on which they had become so dependent, and many died in the process. However, opium never completely left China. In 2003, there were one million registered users, but the numbers today remain unknown.

Conclusion

The Xianfeng Emperor and Empress Dowager Cixi are the first known imperial couple addicted to opium. While Cixi, through an iron will, managed to control her addiction by consuming just enough to keep her going through the day, her husband was not the same. He died of overindulgence, but there are no details preserved that describe his last hours. Opium addiction continued in the next century too, and it stayed within the imperial family. The last empress of Imperial China, Empress Wanrong, is perhaps the perfect image of an opium addict.

Empress Wanrong started consuming opium in small doses as a relaxant during her endless days of captivity in the Forbidden City. As an empress, she wasn't allowed to leave the walls of the palace. As her addiction grew, her behavior changed. Ignored by her husband, she sought compassion and love from other people who surrounded her. She indulged in many affairs, which resulted in a daughter. However, her baby girl was intentionally killed right after birth, as she was an illegitimate princess. Nothing could comfort the empress now except opium. She started consuming more and more of the drug so she could forget her fate in an opium daze. By the time she was imprisoned as a Japanese collaborator by the Communist guerillas, Wanrong was half-mad. In prison, suffering from withdrawal, she often hallucinated and believed she was still an empress at the Forbidden City. She ordered imaginary servants around and played an imaginary organ. She didn't last long in prison. Empress Wanrong died in shame, naked, in a pool of her own bodily fluids.

Many Chinese people shared the same fate as the last empress. Opium was available to all social classes, and if they didn't die from withdrawal, people either died from a drug overdose or were simply tortured and killed by the members of the Communist Party. Ever since its introduction, Chinese rulers tried to ban the opium trade and its use. Even after the Second Opium War, when it was legalized, the effort to suppress its use continued. Various imperial officials tried to raise the taxes on opium, believing that high prices would stop the people from buying it. However, Britain was too powerful an enemy, and China feared retaliation. Many letters to the British prime minister and the royal family were written, in which the Chinese emperor asked why Britain continued to insist on selling the poison to others. They never received an answer, even though it was a very simple one. The money was just too good.

When Britain stopped showing interest in selling opium to China, it wasn't because its politicians suddenly found new morality. It was simply because the domestic production of the drug boomed, pushing the foreign importers out of the picture.

Widespread opium addiction officially ended in China in 1960. Its production continued, but only in high enough quantities to satisfy medicinal use. It took over 150 years for China to get rid of the pestilence imposed upon them by foreign powers. Ironically, the Communist Mao and his followers used the same methods as the Daoguang Emperor and the famous Lin Zexu, which instigated the First Opium War. But there was no British to rebel this time.

Here's another book by Captivating History that you might be interested in

References

Grasso, J. (2015). Modernization and Revolution in China. doi:10.4324/9781315702339

Hanes, W. T., & Sanello, F. (2007). *The Opium Wars: The Addiction of One Empire and the Corruption of Another.* Naperville, IL: Sourcebooks.

Kent, S. K. (2017). *A New History of Britain since 1688: Four Nations and an Empire.* New York: Oxford University Press.

Newsinger, J. (1997). Britain's Opium Wars. *Monthly Review, 49*(5), 35. doi:10.14452/mr-049-05-1997-09_5

Reist, K. (2011). Opium Wars (1839-1842, 1856-1860). *The Encyclopedia of War.* doi:10.1002/9781444338232.wbeow463

Sanello, F., & Hanes, W. T. (2002). *Opium Wars: The Politics and Economics of Addiction.* Naperville, IL: Sourcebooks.

Printed in Great Britain
by Amazon